Increasing Retention: Academic and Student Affairs Administrators in Partnership

Martha McGinty Stodt, *Editor*
Columbia University

William M. Klepper, *Editor*
Trenton State College

NEW DIRECTIONS FOR HIGHER EDUCATION
MARTIN KRAMER, *Editor-in-Chief*
University of California, Berkeley

Number 60, Winter 1987

D0771649

Paperback sourcebooks in
The Jossey-Bass Higher Education Series

Jossey-Bass Inc., Publishers
San Francisco • London

Martha McGinty Stodt, William M. Klepper (eds.).
Increasing Retention: Academic and Student Affairs Administrators in Partnership.
New Directions for Higher Education, no. 60.
Volume XV, number 4.
San Francisco: Jossey-Bass, 1987.

New Directions for Higher Education
Martin Kramer, *Editor-in-Chief*

New Directions for Higher Education is published quarterly by Jossey-Bass Inc., Publishers (publication number USPS 990-880). *New Directions* is numbered sequentially—please order extra copies by sequential number. The volume and issue numbers above are included for the convenience of libraries. Second-class postage paid at San Francisco, California, and at additional mailing offices. POSTMASTER: Send address changes to Jossey-Bass Inc., Publishers, 433 California Street, San Francisco, California 94104.

Editorial correspondence should be sent to the Editor-in-Chief, Martin Kramer, 2807 Shasta Road, Berkeley, California 94708.

Library of Congress Catalog Card Number LC 85-644752

International Standard Serial Number ISSN 0271-0560

International Standard Book Number ISBN 1-55542-948-3

Cover art by WILLI BAUM

Manufactured in the United States of America

Ordering Information

The paperback sourcebooks listed below are published quarterly and can be ordered either by subscription or single copy.

Subscriptions cost $48.00 per year for institutions, agencies, and libraries. Individuals can subscribe at the special rate of $36.00 per year *if payment is by personal check.* (Note that the full rate of $48.00 applies if payment is by institutional check, even if the subscription is designated for an individual.) Standing orders are accepted.

Single copies are available at $11.95 when payment accompanies order. (California, New Jersey, New York, and Washington, D.C., residents please include appropriate sales tax.) For billed orders, cost per copy is $11.95 plus postage and handling.

Substantial discounts are offered to organizations and individuals wishing to purchase bulk quantities of Jossey-Bass sourcebooks. Please inquire.

Please note that these prices are for the academic year 1987–88 and are subject to change without notice. Also, some titles may be out of print and therefore not available for sale.

To ensure correct and prompt delivery, all orders must give either the *name of an individual* or an *official purchase order number.* Please submit your order as follows:

Subscriptions: specify series and year subscription is to begin.
Single Copies: specify sourcebook code (such as, HE1) and first two words of title.

Mail orders for United States and Possessions, Australia, New Zealand, Canada, Latin America, and Japan to:
Jossey-Bass Inc., Publishers
433 California Street
San Francisco, California 94104

Mail orders for all other parts of the world to:
Jossey-Bass Limited
28 Banner Street
London EC1Y 8QE

New Directions for Higher Education Series
Martin Kramer, *Editor-in-Chief*

Contents

Editors' Notes

Interest in student retention is strong and steadily increasing. Research on effective strategies has proliferated, and evidence is mounting that persistence in college is a by-product of excellence in education, the kind of excellence that involves the students with the learning experience and develops their fullest potential. A consortium of twelve schools (American University, Canisius College, University of Delaware, Duquesne University, St. Francis College, Indiana University of Pennsylvania, University of Maryland–Baltimore County, New York Institute of Technology, Ramapo College, Rider College, Rochester Institute of Technology, and Trenton State College) was launched in fall 1984 with the expectation of identifying and then demonstrating practices and programs that promote educational excellence, student development, and retention. In the subsequent two years the consortium schools discovered certain features that are essential for good retention rates. Moreover, they have proved to be congruent with sound educational goals, programs, and practices.

The purpose of this volume is to provide college administrators with fresh, timely, and realistic information about the systematic efforts of a group of institutions to improve their retention rates while retaining high standards of education. In fact, the two processes proved to be mutually reinforcing.

In the first chapter, Stodt reviews the literature both on the impact of college on students and on student retention to demonstrate that the same factors that promote beneficial outcomes from college also promote retention. In addition, the policies and practices that encourage both the cognitive and the affective development of students are consonant with those that encourage persistence in college.

In the second chapter, Stodt presents the rationale for launching the consortium as a collaboration between academic and student affairs. She outlines the progress of schools and describes the key issues and findings that consistently emerged as pivotal in the institutions' effectiveness in retaining students. Stodt served as the director and consultant for the consortium from 1984 to 1986.

The essential role of institutional research in the management of retention is presented in the third chapter by Klepper, Nelson, and Miller. The consortium used the resources of the University of California at Los Angeles's Higher Education Research Institute under the leadership of Alexander W. Astin to structure its research design. Two types of institutional research are offered: one institution's use of the American Council

1

on Education's Cooperative Institutional Research Program (CIRP) surveys and two "in-house" efforts of schools who already had well-conceived institutional research designs.

Chapter Four presents four programs that are exemplary retention strategies for the freshman year. Dunphy describes the College Seminar at Trenton State College over its ten-year history and how nonattendance could serve as an early warning of potential attrition. Miller presents the Mentoring Program at Canisius College, which over six years has proven to enhance student retention and academic performance. Woodruff outlines the Academic Intervention Program at Rider College for conditionally admitted students that has successfully raised the students' semester grade point average to more than 2.0. Finally, Nelson describes how Duquesne University has successfully implemented a new student seminar modeled after the universally popular University 101 Program at the University of South Carolina.

The "at-risk" student is the target group of the four programs described in Chapter Five. Changing demographics indicate that more minority, older, and commuting students will be going to college in the future—student groups that categorically have greater attrition. Sharkey presents the Retention Program for Black Students at the University of Delaware, which is designed to alleviate the disparity between the retention of white and black students. Bischoff, Echols, and Morrison describe the Minority Achievement Program at Ramapo College and its linkage of the college's existing Cooperative Education and Educational Opportunity Program efforts. Northman reports on the advisement program for high-risk adult students at Canisius College that has dramatically increased retention of these students. Lastly, Liebman and Steele outline the Commuter Peer Assistance Program recently begun at the University of Maryland-Baltimore Campus. The freshman students in the program had an attrition rate that was significantly lower than students in a control group.

The concluding chapter by Klepper and Stodt outlines and discusses the benefits of participating in the consortium, beginning with an emphasis on the do's and don't's. The positive outcomes of the consortium experience by the participants has led eight of the twelve schools to continue as the East Coast Consortium. The group has opened its membership to other colleges and universities who choose to bring the academic, administrative, and student affairs staff together in a united effort to improve students' educational experience and thereby encourage their persistence in college.

Martha McGinty Stodt
William M. Klepper
Editors

Martha McGinty Stodt is adjunct professor of business at Columbia University Graduate School of Business and was director of the Intentional Student Development and Retention Consortium.

William M. Klepper is dean of student life, Trenton State College, and serves as coordinator of the Human Relations Department in the School of Arts and Sciences.

Practices and programs that ensure high-quality education also encourage persistence in college.

Educational Excellence as a Prescription for Retention

Martha McGinty Stodt

Colleges and universities today may pursue three major goals that are consistent and mutually reinforcing: quality education, student development, and retention of students. Research studies of student retention and the impact of a college education on students reveal that factors that encourage persistence in college also increase the benefits of a college education. Moreover, these conditions foster student development. Recognition that the same factors support and reinforce the attainment of these ultimate goals motivated twelve colleges and universities to form a consortium in fall 1984. They intended to demonstrate that practices and programs that produce more fully educated graduates also promote persistence in college.

The Rationale

Quality education is here defined as a college experience that yields the benefits described in studies by Feldman and Newcomb (1969), Chickering (1974), Astin (1977), and Bowen (1977)—namely, greater intellectual and interpersonal competence, increased tolerance for racial and cultural differences, and greater satisfaction in career, marriage, and life-style. The

M. M. Stodt, W. M. Klepper (eds.). *Increasing Retention: Academic and Student Affairs Administrators in Partnership.*
New Directions for Higher Education, no. 60. San Francisco: Jossey-Bass, Winter 1987.

factors that produce these outcomes are congruent with those that promote student retention. For example, the power of on-campus residence to involve a student with college, the valuation of student friendships, and the importance of a caring attitude by the faculty and staff were indicated in research long ago (Bolton and Kammeyer, 1967; Heath, 1968; Chickering, 1974). These findings have been corroborated with massive data by the Cooperative Institutional Research Program (CIRP) over the past two decades. Moreover, these conditions were found to correlate positively with student retention (Astin, 1975; Noel, 1978; Beal and Noel, 1980; Aitken, 1982; Noel and others, 1985).

Many educators espouse the full development of the student, affectively as well as cognitively, as a goal for a college education. Here again, policies, programs, and practices that help students to accomplish their developmental tasks are consistent with those that promote persistence in college. The research on student attrition and retention demonstrates that the late adolescent and early adult's struggles with identity issues, career choices, interpersonal competence, and values formation clearly affect student decisions to continue or to complete a college education.

So far little attention has been paid to the fiscal damage, both to the institution and to the individual student, of colleges' recruiting and enrolling students and then failing to supply the kinds of academic and social support that would enable them to maintain attendance. Similarly, the cost of failed aspirations and efforts for students who drop out represents formidable human waste. The toll is particularly heavy among nontraditional students who were recruited to fill empty seats in college classrooms and who were then often left to flounder and fail in an unfamiliar system. Ironically, their needs have differed from those of traditional students not as much in kind as in amount. For example, residence on campus, student friendships, and faculty-student interaction have emerged as especially powerful "retainers" in recent literature about minority students in college (Fleming, 1984). We know how to help high-risk students to succeed. Schools must decide whether to apply this knowledge.

Higher Education Goals: Ultimate and Intermediate

The attainment of the three ultimate goals—quality education, student development, and student retention—depends mainly on two components: the development of certain cognitive and affective conditions within students and the institutional factors that foster these intra-student processes.

Intra-Student Processes. Students' satisfaction with their college experiences and their involvement with their institutions have been described as highly significant in the literature discussing both the benefits of a college education and student retention. Satisfaction with college is especially important because it correlates more with institutional characteristics than with any other determinant and is more amenable to institutional efforts. Student "involvement" was defined by Astin (1984b) as the quantity and quality of the physical and psychological energy that the student invests in the college experience, whether it takes the form of absorption in academic work, participation in extracurricular activities, or interaction with the faculty.

The institutional factors that appear in the literature most frequently as contributors to satisfaction with college and to student involvement are student interaction with the faculty, the formation of student friendships, and residence on campus. Administrative arrangements such as financial aid and on-campus employment have also increased student involvement. Understandably, student involvement in college activities increases student satisfaction with college just as participation in college activities increases student involvement with the institution.

Another intra-student process noted through decades of research and observations of students is the balance of challenge and support for the student. Sanford (1969, 1967) established that unless a certain amount of disequilibrium with "held beliefs" occurs in the student, change and growth do not occur. However, the stress caused by such dissonance must not be insurmountable. The environment must supply sufficient support for the new concepts to be assimilated and absorbed at a higher level of complexity.

Historically, challenges to students' attitudes and habits have occurred through exposure to new ideas in courses and college activities, exposure to diverse beliefs of faculty, staff, and peers, and exposure to new roles that require new skills and an altered self-image. This vital process is threatened in the current scene for many commuting students. Greater access to higher education has been provided for them, but the lack of disruption to their accustomed lives may actually diminish the amount of challenge to their values and life-styles. Support for students as they confront change has been supplied by interaction with the faculty, a social support system among peers, staff resources, faculty and staff "role models," and human development programs that are socially and emotionally educational. The need for such support has proven to be even more crucial for nontraditional students.

A fourth intra-student process is the estimation of value received from attending college: The result is "perceived pay-off." We now recognize that our students must be convinced as consumers that their goals will be met if they attend our schools—we call this activity "recruiting." Retaining students, however, is related to another concept called "post-purchase marketing." Students do not buy a four-year contract culminating in a degree; they buy one semester at a time as they continue their enrollment.

College administrators have learned that we must meet the wants and expectations of the student consumer. They are less skilled at assuring students that their needs, both immediate and future, are being met. To do this, they must help students recognize the ways in which their investment is paying off, by indicating the benefits gained from a given course, contacts made at the college, supportive services, and activities that prepare them for the "real" world.

The Institutional Factors. The ways in which colleges and universities manage their institutional resources are the methods by which they achieve the intermediate goals of student satisfaction, involvement with college, a balance of challenge and support, and perception of payoff (see Figure 1). The institutional factors fall into three domains: the academic, the administrative policies, and student life on campus.

Academic Domain

Academia generally agrees that the transmission of knowledge and the development of the intellect are the major purposes of higher education. And recently, some retention research shows a higher correlation between academic performance and persistence in college (Aitken, 1982; Spady, 1970). Conversely, students name poor academic advising and boredom with courses as the leading reasons for dropping out (Beal and Noel, 1980). In response to growing awareness of these influences, faculty development programs have burgeoned with emphasis not only on improving teaching skills but also on acquiring more diversity of teaching tech-

Figure 1. Synergy of College and Student

Ultimate Goals		
Student Development	Retention	Quality Education

Student Factors that Promote Ultimate Goals			
Perceived Payoff	Student Satisfaction	Student Involvement	Challenge and Support

Institutional Factors that Promote Intermediate Goals		
Academic Domain	Administrative Policies and Practices	Student Life on Campus
Instruction		*Friendships*
Faculty		*Participation in Activities*
Academic Advising		*Assistance with*
Learning Supports		*Developmental Tasks*

niques in order to accommodate students' different learning styles. And the importance of academic advising has received so much attention that it has arisen as a new profession with its own professional association, journal, and workshops in abundance.

Faculty-student interaction emerged in earlier research (Feldman and Newcomb, 1969; Astin, 1977) as a leading factor in student satisfaction with college and has appeared again as a powerful retention factor (Pascarella and Terenzini, 1977, 1980; Beal and Noel, 1980). One should note, however, that the interaction students value most continues to be that which occurs *outside* the class. In recent years Endo has focused specifically on the nature of faculty-student interaction and its relative effectiveness. Endo and Harpel (1982) have found that informal contact, in which faculty members develop more friendly relationships with students and exhibit a personal and broad concern with their emotional and cognitive growth, has more influence not only on students' personal and social outcomes but also on their intellectual gains.

A relatively recent development in the academic domain—the rise and spread of learning support programs—has had a significant effect on student retention. These centers have shown results in keeping poorly prepared students in college, not only because they assist with academic skills but also because they provide emotional support (Kemerer, Baldridge, and Green, 1982; Astin, 1984a). Moreover, students in general are less confident of themselves academically today (Astin, 1984a) and can be expected to benefit from learning support programs.

Administrative Policies and Practices

Academic administrators may have little control over the size and type of their institution, but they do have some latitude about certain administrative factors that have demonstrable success in involving students with college. For example, financial aid that permits students to attend school full-time rather than part-time or that assists part-time students so that they need to work fewer hours enables them to invest more time in learning activities. Student employment *on* rather than *off* campus also promotes involvement with the institution. Residence on campus, especially when living arrangements encourage student interaction, is a major asset. Institutions lacking campus residences can allocate space and resources for programs and services that offer commuter students some of the advantages of residential life in surrogate form.

Administrators and their policies throughout the institution must show awareness of their impact on students, whether the staff function is collecting student data, tracking student progress, treating students courteously, or providing interventions when problems occur.

Student Life on Campus

The intermediate goals—satisfaction with college, involvement, a balance of challenge and support, and perception of payoff—can be used as a gauge by which we measure the nonacademic programs and services that we offer our students. The research literature presents considerable evidence about the nonacademic experiences that foster these intra-student processes.

According to early research by Wallace (1966), Heath (1968), Feldman and Newcomb (1969), and the CIRP data of twenty years, student friendships are a leading influence on student satisfaction and involvement with college. Current retention research (Spady, 1970; Lacy, 1978; Terenzini and Pascarella, 1980) identifies peer interaction as a strong factor in students' intellectual and personal development. Furthermore, the dissonance of diverse viewpoints, habits, and mores provided by peers is a major source of challenge for students away from home. Similarly, peers are the main source of support at college for most students. As for the fourth intra-student process, perceived payoff, students may not go to college specifically to acquire friends, but numerous studies show that they perceive its value for that purpose while there. As Chickering states, "A student's most important teacher is another student. Friends and reference groups filter and modulate the messages from the larger student culture. They amplify or attenuate the force of the curriculum, faculty, parental rules, institutional regulations. They can trump the best teacher's ace and stalemate the most thoughtful or agile dean. These relationships with close friends and peer groups, or subcultures, are primary forces influencing student development in college, and all seven vectors of change are affected" (1969, p. 253).

According to Astin (1977, 1984b, 1985) and others, a second positive force is heavy participation in some college activity—not just studies, but clubs and organizations, student government, and athletics. Anything that brings students to campus often, keeps them on campus, and connects them with persons of mutual interests—whether faculty, students, or staff—promotes student satisfaction with college. Participation obviously involves them with the college; and participation provides both the challenge of others' ideas and support from the reference group. Moreover, the activity must offer a payoff of some kind or the student would not be active.

Little research has been done that can offer empirical evidence that assistance to students with their developmental tasks promotes the intra-student processes discussed here. The idea, however, has "face validity." College programs and services that help students to become more autonomous, recognize and accept interdependence, acquire interpersonal competence, identify appropriate career choices, and develop a value system can only increase their satisfaction and involvement with the institution. Challenge and support are implicit in the process, and payoff for future life is easily perceived. Furthermore, students drop out of college more often for personal than for academic problems.

The foregoing logic suggests that student affairs administrators may assess, plan, and then evaluate each student service and program by measuring how much it contributes to the formation of student friendships, to participation in some meaningful college activities, and to assistance with developmental tasks. Furthermore, they may ask whether it does so at a minimal, acceptable, or maximal level. These elements are not the whole picture, but they do offer useful indicators of effectiveness. In fact, to some extent they provide a formula.

To illustrate this approach, let us examine a hypothetical college's orientation program for entering students: Is the program minimal, in that it merely introduces the student to the school by offering information about the institution—its personnel, services, history, regulations? Is it more acceptable, in that it also provides time and situations in which students can initiate friendships and explore issues such as the relevance of college major to career choice—which begins the process of feeling included and identified with the college? Or is the orientation program maximal, in that it accomplishes all of these tasks and also addresses students' developmental tasks by offering ongoing seminars that assist with adjustment to college, promote independence by encouraging new ideas and new roles, provide support groups, explore career choices, increase interpersonal skills, and explore value systems?

Similarly, each aspect of student life on campus can be evaluated from the perspective of its strength in fostering student friendships, participation in college life, and assistance with personal development, which in turn would promote student satisfaction and involvement with college and contribute to the balance of challenge and support and a sense of payoff. As the institution manages its resources to attain these intermediate goals, it simultaneously approaches the ultimate goals of quality education, student development, and student retention.

The Formation of the Consortium

Findings from a wide range of research were construed to form the premise that the same forces that augment the value of a college education and foster student development also encourage persistence in college. The congruence among these bodies of research was not surprising, but it was exciting because it presented evidence that our major goals were mutually reinforcing and even synergistic. With this premise as the guide, a consortium of twelve colleges and universities formed to demonstrate that philosophies and practices that intentionally promote the full development of students also produce the maximum benefits of a college education and at the same time increase student retention.

References

Aitken, N. "College Student Performance, Satisfaction, and Retention." *Journal of Higher Education,* 1982, *53* (1), 32–50.

Astin, A. W. *Preventing Students from Dropping Out.* San Francisco: Jossey-Bass, 1975.

Astin, A. W. *Four Critical Years: Effects of College on Beliefs, Attitudes, and Knowledge.* San Francisco: Jossey-Bass, 1977.

Astin, A. W. "A Look at Pluralism in the Contemporary Student Population." *NASPA Journal,* 1984a, *21* (3), 2–11.

Astin, A. W. "Student Involvement: A Developmental Theory for Higher Education." *Journal of College Personnel,* 1984b, *25* (4), 297–308.

Astin, A. W. *Achieving Educational Excellence: A Critical Assessment of Priorities and Practices in Higher Education.* San Francisco: Jossey-Bass, 1985.

Beal, P. E., and Noel, L. *What Works in Student Retention.* Iowa City, Iowa: American College Testing Program and National Center for Higher Education Management Systems, 1980.

Bolton, C., and Kammeyer, K. *The University Student: A Study of Student Behavior and Values.* New Haven, Conn.: College and University Press, 1967.

Bowen, H. *Investment in Learning: The Individual and Social Value of American Higher Education.* San Francisco: Jossey-Bass, 1977.

Chickering, A. W. *Education and Identity.* San Francisco: Jossey-Bass, 1969.

Chickering, A. W. *Commuting Versus Resident Students: Overcoming Educational Inequities of Living Off Campus.* San Francisco: Jossey-Bass, 1974.

Endo, J., and Harpel, R. "The Effect of Student-Faculty Interaction on Students' Educational Outcomes." *Research in Higher Education,* 1982, *16,* 115–138.

Feldman, K. A., and Newcomb, T. M. *The Impact of College on Students.* San Francisco: Jossey-Bass, 1969.

Fleming, J. *Blacks in College: A Comparative Study of Students' Success in Black and in White Institutions.* San Francisco: Jossey-Bass, 1984.

Heath, D. H. *Growing Up in College: Liberal Education and Maturity.* San Francisco: Jossey-Bass, 1968.

Kemerer, F., Baldridge, V., and Green, K. *Strategies for Effective Enrollment Management.* Washington, D.C.: American Association of State Colleges and Universities, 1982.

Lacy, W. "Interpersonal Relationships as Mediators or Structural Effects: College Student Socialization in a Traditional and an Experimental University Environment." *Sociology of Education,* 1978, *51,* 201–211.

Noel, L. (ed.). *Reducing the Dropout Rate.* New Directions for Student Services, no. 3. San Francisco: Jossey-Bass, 1978.

Noel, L., Levitz, R., Saluri, D., and Associates. *Increasing Student Retention: Effective Programs and Practices for Reducing the Dropout Rate.* San Francisco: Jossey-Bass, 1985.

Pascarella, E., and Terenzini, P. "Patterns of Student-Faculty Informal Interaction Beyond the Classroom and Voluntary Freshman Attrition." *Journal of Higher Education,* 1977, *48,* 540–552.

Pascarella, E., and Terenzini, P. "Student-Faculty Informal Contact and College Outcomes." *Review of Educational Research,* 1980, *50,* 545–595.

Sanford, N. *The American College*. New York: Wiley, 1967.

Sanford, N. *Self and Society*. New York: Atherton Press, 1969.

Spady, W. "Dropouts from Higher Education: An Interdisciplinary Review and Synthesis." *Interchange*, 1970, *1*, 64–85.

Terenzini, P., and Pascarella, E. "Student-Faculty Relationships and Freshman Year Educational Outcomes: A Further Investigation." *Journal of College Student Personnel*, 1980, *27*, 521–528.

Wallace, W. *Student Culture*. Chicago: Aldine, 1966.

Martha McGinty Stodt is adjunct professor of business at Columbia University Graduate School of Business and was director of the Intentional Student Development and Retention Consortium.

The preeminent requirement for successful student retention
is cooperation between academic and student affairs domains.

Intentional Student Development and Retention

Martha McGinty Stodt

The synergy among quality education, student development, and retention as goals for an educational institution provided the impetus for a group of colleges and universities to form a consortium. The group addressed the crucial issue of retention but did so on the assumption that retention is primarily a by-product of educational excellence. Educational excellence, furthermore, includes elements that foster the development of students affectively as well as cognitively—which the consortium called "intentional student development."

The preeminent requirement for success along all three paths, clearly indicated by the various bodies of research, was collaboration throughout the institution and especially between the academic and student affairs domains. Therefore, membership in the consortium was contingent on the expectation that such cooperation could be attained. A number of chief student affairs officers with a solid commitment to student development as a goal for higher education were invited to a two-day institute at Teachers College, Columbia University, entitled "Intentional Student Development as a Prescription for Retention." Attendance by one or more suitable academic representatives was also expected from each institution. In addition, institutions were asked to provide data based on Astin's Worksheets for Predicting Chances of Dropping Out

M. M. Stodt, W. M. Klepper (eds.). *Increasing Retention: Academic and Student Affairs Administrators in Partnership.*
New Directions for Higher Education, no. 60. San Francisco: Jossey-Bass, Winter 1987.

15

(Astin, 1975), which would be processed to forecast attrition. Also the Cooperative Institutional Research Program's (CIRP) entering student and follow-up surveys would establish a student data base by which the effect of demographic characteristics and the efficacy of the institution's efforts could be measured in subsequent years.

The Institute

On the first day of the institute, the rationale and design for a consortium were presented. Institutional attrition forecasts were distributed and interpreted, and the use of a computerized version of Astin's attrition worksheet for institutional research purposes was introduced. Participants met in teams to share their concerns, problems, and successes with student retention, and intentional versus ad hoc efforts were contrasted.

On the second day of the institute, participants focused on organizing the consortium. Teams from similar types of institutions (public, private, small college, university) met to:

- Identify each institution's programs and services that seemed to be most conducive to student growth—and explore why they were effective
- Select specific aspects of student life that could be improved for attrition-prone groups
- Share ideas and tactics for improving these aspects
- Plan a strategy for obtaining administrative cooperation and institutional support for the project.

The original composition of the consortium included five community colleges. During the institute the circumstances and concerns of the two-year colleges emerged as sufficiently different from those of the four-year institutions to require a separate enterprise.

The Consortium

The consortium members were urged to take the following steps in order to achieve institutional collaboration: First, they were instructed to form a strategy committee or task force, preferably including the word *retention* in its name in order to benefit from the term's motivational value. The unit would contain members from both the academic and the student affairs areas, since a partnership between them would be essential for success. Second, members were told to inform their institutions about its attrition forecast, the consortium, and its objectives. Third, after identifying attrition-prone groups or areas as targets, members were advised to enlist the staff or constituency of targets in the project and to publicize their plans.

As a "retention" committee, they would next develop a strategy utilizing the research findings in our rationale to improve the target areas or target population programs and services. Measures to overcome obstacles and obtain cooperation needed to be included. Finally, after actions were taken as a result of the retention committee's plans, they would systematically collect evidence of results and disseminate them throughout the institution in order to obtain increasing collaboration. Most important, they were to demonstrate the congruences among programs and practices that promoted educational excellence, student development, and retention.

In November 1984 twelve of the fifteen four-year colleges represented at the institute formed the Intentional Student Development and Retention Consortium, and it began to function that winter. We had anticipated that enthusiasm would fade and efforts diminish back at the "home" institutions unless a consortium director corresponded with representatives at the respective campuses, visited each school annually as a consultant, and arranged follow-up meetings for the consortium schools. Consequently, this role was incorporated into the consortium design. Immediately after the institute, the director followed up with letters and press releases to the member institutions. Shortly thereafter, she requested progress reports from the campuses and suggested guidelines for those reports.

On-Campus Consultations. Campus visits began in late February. The agenda for each visit was planned by the director with each institution's consortium representative and was adapted to the needs of that situation. In general, however, the visits of the director provided an impetus to increase cooperation among the institutional components as they prepared for the day's consultation. In addition, the campus visits helped to identify strong programs and services, to consolidate ambiguous, disorganized plans, and to develop methods for strengthening weak areas. The consultations also generated increased enthusiasm for the institution's efforts. We had been convinced that the director as a consultant must have both administrative and faculty background and status in order to have credibility with all constituencies. Our experience validated this prediction.

On a typical day of consultation in the first year, the director would meet with whatever "retention" officer or committee the administration had designated—which varied from one individual to a single retention committee to dual retention committees. The meeting was generally viewed as a progress report on the institution's retention efforts and served to integrate efforts and to identify both strengths and problem areas within the institution's strategy. Some institutions' retention efforts seemed to be in initial stages, while others' were well underway.

The consultant then had conferences with the person in charge of institutional research, with staff and faculty members who were perceived as obstacles or as effective supporters of the retention effort, and with persons in charge of significant institutional areas, such as commuter affairs, student activities, residential life, and special programs for "high-risk" students. Since academic advisement is such a crucial element in student progress, the consultant met with key persons working in this area. In the first year of the consortium the consultant always conferred with the chief student affairs officer, frequently with the chief academic officer, and occasionally with the president of the institution. The day usually concluded with a wrap-up session with the consortium representatives in which the consultant summarized her impressions on the status of the consortium's strategy at that institution.

After the campus visit the director followed up with a "diagnostic" letter to the campus consortium representative (and sometimes to other individuals such as a provost). In those letters she attempted to reinforce strengths observed at the institution and to emphasize suggestions for improvements that had been discussed at the time of the visit.

Follow-Up Consortium Meetings. At a regional meeting of consortium representatives the following June, Kenneth Green, associate director of CIRP and the Higher Education Research Institute of UCLA, stressed the importance of annual conferences and the need to involve the chief executive officer of the consortium institutions. Mr. Green also provided invaluable suggestions to our consortium. As a result, we conducted a 1985 fall conference at Trenton State College and made a special effort to have presidents attend. Although only a few presidents were able to attend, the consortium schools were well represented, and the meeting was featured in an article in the *New York Times* (Friendly, 1985) on our retention strategies.

One presentation at the 1985 consortium meeting was an update on the literature pertaining to our goals of retention, quality education, and student development.

New Developments in Literature and Research. In the year following the launching of our consortium, major publications in higher education reaffirmed our analysis of the literature on which we based the consortium's rationale. Three main emphases were further corroboration of the importance of student involvement to increasing learning, the validity of the same institutional factors in promoting learning and persistence in college among minority students, and additional support for the importance of meeting students' developmental needs as an aid to retention.

Probably the single most influential publication was *Involvement in Learning* (1984), the report of the two-year study group established by the National Institute of Education to make recommendations to improve undergraduate education. Of the twenty-seven recommendations, certain ones were particularly relevant to our consortium tenets, such as:

1. College administrators should reallocate faculty and other institutional resources to increase service to first- and second-year undergraduate students (which are the most crucial years for survival as a student) (p. 25).

2. The faculty should make use of active modes of teaching and require that students take more responsibility for their learning (p. 27).

3. All colleges should offer a systematic program of guidance and advisement that involves students from matriculation through graduation, and all should participate in the system (p. 31).

4. Academic and student service administrators should provide adequate fiscal support, space, and recognition to existing cocurricular programs and activities for the purposes of maximizing student involvement, including part-time and commuter students (p. 35).

5. College officials responsible for faculty personnel decisions should increase the weight given to *teaching,* and they should improve the means of assessing teaching effectiveness (p. 59).

In addition, this publication emphasized the need to measure student growth in learning and development and to utilize the results as a valid indicator of institutional quality. Moreover, the measurement of the intervening educational experiences and their specific effects on students was advocated.

Astin's *Achieving Educational Excellence* (1985) reinforced the conclusion that educational excellence represents the pursuit of intellectual and personal development of students as its fundamental purpose. In what he called the talent development view, "a high-quality institution is one that facilitates maximum growth among its students and faculty and that can document that growth through appropriate assessment procedures" (p. 77). Astin proceeded to develop more firmly and comprehensively than ever before the premise that the involvement of the student with the educational experience is the key to effective learning. He also addressed all aspects of institutional life and offered his views of how the student can be engaged: for example, by more active modes of teaching, curricular innovation, student-faculty contact, and skillful academic advising. Astin attributed some of the persisting problems in higher education to the failure of institutions to implement these findings. This book represents an excellent "text" for leaders of academic institutions seeking to produce fully educated human beings while simultaneously maintaining student enrollment.

Another major development following the formation of the consortium was the emerging body of research about minority students and their experiences in higher education. Previous research cited here might be justifiably criticized as based primarily on the college experience of traditional student populations. Fleming's (1984) four-year, multifaceted study of black and white students, however, presented evidence that meaningful friendships, active participation in campus life, and interaction with teachers may be more influential than superior institutional facilities and resources. These factors were more conducive to both personal growth and academic achievement. She concluded that black students made more progress in certain predominantly black colleges precisely because they had more of these kinds of experiences.

Bennett and Bean (1984) report studies indicating that positive interracial contact experiences prior to and during college attendance not only reduce trauma and alienation but also increase persistence in college among black students in predominantly white schools. Neither high standardized test scores nor high grades in college were good predictors of college satisfaction or persistence. Donovan (1984), in a study of low-income black youth found that actual experiences in college were more significant in determining persistence than background variables such as family and individual characteristics, and Badu and Butler (1985) also found that family background did not predict academic achievement for low-income minority students. Other studies of nontraditional students, such as those of Pratt and Gentemann (1984) and Weidman and White (1984) showed the power of noncognitive variables like motivation to encourage persistence, regardless of background obstacles. Such studies suggest that artful and constructive management of nontraditional students' college experiences is not only possible but perhaps essential in order to prevent attrition.

A third useful development subsequent to the formation of the consortium has been corroboration of the importance of assisting students with personal and often-times nonacademic issues. Much retention research has contained what are called "social integration" variables (Spady, 1970; Tinto, 1975; Pascarella, 1980). Astin's extensive research consistently reveals nonacademic dimensions as contributors to the benefits of a college education, and evidence is mounting that students require much more than courses and teachers to persist in college.

The latest and most complete report on retention by Noel and others (1985) is replete with this theme. To illustrate, Anderson in Chapter Two described the normal requirements for completing an academic degree, which can be viewed as "obstacles," depending on the institution's standards and the student's level of preparation. These impediments are followed by negative external forces that "tend to push a student out of college or at least militate against academic success" (p. 47). All nine forces are nonacademic, such as housing or transportation problems, work, family, and social demands. Ten internal negative forces are offered, which the author groups into two categories: (1) self-defeating perceptions and behavior patterns and (2) confusion or indecision. Anderson then distinguishes between institutional factors that promote persistence and those that foster academic achievement, which he sees as interrelated but not

identical. Again, those identified as persistence factors were all nonacademic programs and services, such as individuals who take a personal
interest in students, financial support, adequate orientation programs,
appropriate counseling services, and support systems that make students
feel a part of the college community. This is the type of evidence that has
appeared in most publications about retention, whether they be research
reports or descriptive articles. Clearly, students' academic progress is integrated with and contingent on the practical and emotional ingredients of
their daily lives—and their colleges must pay heed to these realities.

The Consortium Issues and Findings

In addition to the annual conference, the consortium school representatives also met in smaller, informal meetings during which they
exchanged ideas and made progress reports, and the consortium director
carried out the second year of campus consultations. During these two
years certain assumptions were tested and conclusions were formed. Other
impressions, no less convincing, grew from the experiences we shared.
Although in these two years we were unable to acquire enough sym-
metry of institutional research among our twelve consortium schools to
present empirical evidence of our outcomes, certain obstacles and solu-
tions emerged consistently enough to suggest patterns of applicability.

Partnership. Based on the foregoing survey of literature and years
of professional experience, we were convinced that both the academic
and the student affairs domains of college life were essential to an excellent education and to the kinds of satisfaction and support that would
encourage students to persist through college.

The mounting concern in colleges and universities over maintaining their enrollments was indeed giving rise to special efforts at retention,
and at first administrators and faculty members were apparently unaware
that the same factors that produced quality education also promoted
retention. As a result of this oversight, chief executives tended to follow
one of three courses: (1) to appoint a retention coordinator or enrollment
manager and assign to that person the responsibility for developing and
implementing strategies to cope with retention at that institution, (2) to
designate the student affairs staff as responsible for retaining students,
and (3) to establish an academic task force to study the problem and
make recommendations.

We found all three patterns in our twelve institutions. At least the
leaders of our schools were aware of retention as an issue and had taken
some kind of action. In some institutions hapless individuals, as retention
designees, were struggling by persuasion or exhortation to awaken their
colleagues to the need for policies and practices that would improve the
retention of students as well as the quality of education. (They could not

apply sanctions because they were without authority!) In other schools chief student affairs officers were striving to bring together representatives from other facets of the institution in a sort of volunteer effort to address the problem. In some institutions separate retention groups, from the institutional staff and from the faculty, were working in parallel formation, with little if any collaboration.

Fortunately, a few presidents moved swiftly to appoint retention task forces with institutionwide representation. Not surprisingly, this collective responsibility produced more comprehensive and active retention strategies. In fact, we viewed the establishment of joint accountability between the academic and student affairs domains as the foremost step toward improving retention. It was a concrete sign of progress when partnership-style retention committees had evolved on most campuses by the second year of the consortium's existence. Otherwise, all schools revealed "pockets" of endeavor on the part of conscientious, talented staff and faculty members, but these efforts obviously lacked the impact of a broader institutional commitment.

Concomitantly, the institutional community had to recognize and accept responsibility for the effect the vast majority of employees had on the students' relationships to the school and indirectly on their education. Even a dedicated retention committee could not succeed if "front-line" staff members performed their services rudely or inefficiently and alienated students.

Role of the Chief Executive. Implicit in the tenet just mentioned is the leadership shown by the chief executive of the institution. Kenneth Green, our consultant, emphasized that retention must be high and visible on the agenda of the president of the institution in order for movement to occur with the institution. We found that it was important not only for presidents to recognize the need for joint academic and student affairs accountability but they also had to speak with the college community about the significance of retention and its financial and curricular ramifications, support the need for student data acquisition and dissemination, and demonstrate in the institutional budget a commitment to meeting students' needs. We cannot report a causal relationship or statistical correlations between the advocacy of the president and the institution's progress in both educational excellence and student retention. We did observe, however, that the most concerted and widespread efforts and the highest institutional morale seemed to derive from this kind of stance by the chief administration.

Institutional Research. One of the major aspirations of the consortium was to verify with empirical evidence our premise that the same institutional factors supported quality education, student development, and retention. It was therefore imperative for our participating institutions to have a student data base against which institutional efforts could be measured. From inception we pressured our schools to develop a system if they did not have one.

Although all institutions had a staff member or members in charge of institutional research, they exhibited a wide range of capability. A few schools already had well-conceived institutional research designs and an enthusiastic staff. Most of the consortium schools were engaged in strategic planning and were learning how essential accurate and accessible data about students are to the process. For many schools, however, considerable "gearing up" was needed for effectiveness. For example, some schools had collected masses of student data via newly acquired technology but lacked either the staff time or the skills to analyze the information into a useful data flow. Others conducted research in an ad hoc or laissez-faire manner so that the various bodies of information were neither coordinated nor disseminated in ways suitable for institutional applications. In some instances, individual staff members or professors outside of the research office provided the most relevant information.

We emphasized the importance of the research function throughout our consortium efforts. We did observe progress in most of our consortium schools in the collection, analysis, and dissemination of information about their students and their college life. The institutions' ability to forecast, plan, and evaluate was of course strengthened. The power of carefully formulated, rigorously assembled, and cogently presented institutional research is demonstrated in Chapter Three by several institutional models from consortium participants.

Faculty-Student Relationships. The crucial significance of faculty and student relationships, both inside and outside of class, was emphasized at every opportunity by the consortium director on campus visits. In conferences with presidents and deans and in meetings, formal and informal, with faculty groups she cited research evidence on the effect of this variable on students' educational experience and its impact on students' persistence in college.

Unfailingly, the lack of "reward" in the academic system both for time spent with students and for the quality of relationships with students was cited as the major deterrent. In the perceptions of both faculty members and administrators, standards for tenure and promotion have been altered little, if any, by current recognition of the importance of faculty attitudes and behavior toward students. As more than one president or dean stated, "What would it matter if I changed? The recommendation for tenure would never even get out of the department!" Although defensiveness and closed minds continue to exist, we also found many teachers with broad concern for their students' welfare and progress on our campuses. These were easily identified by students and colleagues. Furthermore, dialogue among teachers about both the responsibility to motivate students and more active teaching models is happening.

Academic Advising. Although poor academic advising has emerged as the leading reason given by students for dropping out of college, this aspect of the academic program seemed to be the most intractable in our schools. Although some of our institutions had invested rhetoric and even funds in training programs and staff, the old advisement systems generally remained entrenched. Several of the schools, however, had established special programs for high-risk students, and they had demonstrated the power of well-executed academic advisement. Ironically, those students were receiving superior educational attention, whereas the average and superior students were more often left with the minimal value of routine academic advisement. The usual response to this point was that the latter two categories of students do not need more attention, but this attitude does not account for the high attrition rate among many of the brightest students or for the fact that the under-prepared students in the special advisement program often "catch up" and even surpass students without deficits upon entrance. (An example of this kind of program will be presented in the section of Chapter Five called "Advisement Program for High-Risk Adult Students at Canisius College.")

In our experience the lack of progress in this area can be attributed to two unresolved issues: who should do the advising (in most schools all faculty members continued to be required to advise, or to insist upon advising, without commitment to an effective performance) and the lack of either intrinsic and extrinsic rewards for advisement. The proliferation of activities in higher education pertaining to academic advising in the last decade has produced a body of professional skills that could well meet the needs of all students. In our judgment, however, they will not permeate institutional practice until this function is incorporated into the academic reward system.

Student Development Programs. When the chief executive implemented an institutionwide effort to increase retention, it inevitably contained efforts to improve the educational experience of students. One component among our consortium schools was the instigation of ongoing programs that systematically addressed the needs of students, particularly those of entering students. These programs were extensive orientation programs, mentoring programs, freshman seminars, and various types of systems that tracked the progress of students and provided interventions when needed. In fact, this type of program was sometimes launched by dedicated faculty and staff members in schools where no institution-wide effort existed.

The paramount feature of these special programs was that they attended to both the affective and the cognitive development of students. They focused on social and emotional needs as well as on academic tasks. The goals of these programs were multifaceted. For example, a well-designed orientation program initiates the student's involvement with the college, assists with adjustment, fosters college friendships and interaction with faculty, and explores the student's career choices. Mentoring programs were usually geared toward these same goals with a format that follows up on students and solves incipient problems. (Two such programs and their impact on retention are presented in Chapter Four, in the sections called "The Mentoring Program at Canisius College" and "Developing an Extended Orientation Course.")

In our experience, programs of this nature encompassed students' needs at college more than any others. Consequently, they were most able to involve students, to challenge and support them, and to help them see the advantages they were gaining from attending that particular college. In this setting, personal or academic problems that lead to attrition could be discovered, treated, and often resolved before they became insurmountable. As the consortium continues, we predict that this kind of educational program for entering students will be the hallmark of institutional progress toward the goals of quality education, student development, and retention.

Communication. The function of communication is implicit in some of the foregoing themes, but its importance requires specific attention. The benefits of the most elaborate retention strategy, carefully executed institutional research, and dedicated staff and faculty enterprises will be greatly diminished if their existence is unrecognized within the academic community. The flow of information among the various components of the institution about obstacles overcome and triumphs achieved, such as the percentage points of gains in student performance or retention, produces a synergism of collaboration, high morale, and success.

One of the purposes of forming the consortium was to extend this kind of communication among our participating schools. We anticipated the benefit of sharing ideas, materials, problems, and success stories. We achieved this goal through the consortium director as a conduit and by our semiannual meetings. It can be no coincidence that similar kinds of programs and strategies evolved on the respective campuses. For example, at the inception of the consortium, only one member institution had developed a comprehensive program to address the needs of its black students and thus increase their retention. In the second year of the consortium other participants were initiating similar programs, assisted by the model of this institution's strategy. (This program is described in Chapter Five.) The value of communication is further illustrated by the fact that several of the consortium schools requested at the conclusion of its scheduled two years that the consortium continue to function. They have committed themselves to its support financially and professionally; they have extended membership to other institutions and are functioning today.

26

References

Anderson, E. "Forces Influencing Student Persistence and Achievement." In L. Noel, R. Levitz, D. Saluri, and Associates (eds.), *Increasing Student Retention: Effective Programs and Practices for Reducing the Dropout Rate.* San Francisco: Jossey-Bass, 1985.

Astin, A. W. *Preventing Students from Dropping Out.* San Francisco: Jossey-Bass, 1975.

Astin, A. W. *Achieving Educational Excellence: A Critical Assessment of Priorities and Practices in Higher Education.* San Francisco: Jossey-Bass, 1985.

Badu, Y., and Butler, O. "Assessing the Impact of College: A Follow-up Survey of Low-Income Minority Graduates." *NAPW Journal,* 1985, *2,* 25-45.

Bennett, C., and Bean, J. "A Conceptual Model of Black Student Attrition at a Predominantly White University." *Journal of Educational Equity and Leadership,* 1984, *4* (3), 173-188.

Donovan, R. "Path Analysis of a Theoretical Model of Persistence in Higher Education Among Low-Income Black Youths." *Research in Higher Education,* 1984, *21* (3), 243-259.

Fleming, J. *Blacks in College: A Comparative Study of Students' Success in Black and in White Institutions.* San Francisco: Jossey-Bass, 1984.

Friendly, J. "Preventing Dropouts: Will Personal Touch Prevent College Dropouts?" *New York Times,* Education Section, November 26, 1985, p. 1.

Noel, L., Levitz, R., Saluri, D., and Associates. *Increasing Student Retention: Effective Programs and Practices for Reducing the Dropout Rate.* San Francisco: Jossey-Bass, 1985.

Pascarella, E. "Student-Faculty Informal Contact and College Outcomes." *Review of Educational Research,* 1980, *50,* 545-595.

Pratt, L., and Gentemann, K. "Predicting Academic Retention Among Population Subgroups: The Use of Non-Cognitive Predictors." Paper presented at Association for Institutional Research, Fort Worth, Texas, May 1984.

Spady, W. "Dropouts from Higher Education: An Interdisciplinary Review and Synthesis." *Interchange,* 1970, *1,* 64-85.

Study Group on Conditions of Excellence in American Higher Education. *Involvement in Learning: Realizing the Potential of American Higher Education.* Washington, D.C.: National Institute of Education, 1984.

Tinto, J. V. "Dropout from Higher Education: A Theoretical Synthesis of Recent Research." *Review of Educational Research,* 1975, *45,* 89-125.

Weidman, J., and White, R. "Postsecondary 'High Tech' Training for Women on Welfare: Correlates of Program Completion." Paper presented at American Educational Research Association, New Orleans, La., April 1984.

Martha McGinty Stodt is adjunct professor of business at Columbia University Graduate School of Business and was director of the Intentional Student Development and Retention Consortium.

*Information about students' characteristics and their
perceptions of their educational experience allow
institutions to predict their risk of attrition.*

The Role of Institutional
Research in Retention

*William M. Klepper, John E. Nelson,
Thomas E. Miller*

Pascarella, in *Studying Student Attrition* (1982), noted that it is seldom
enough for the institutional researcher to acquire a general sense of the
existing research literature. He and his colleagues then addressed the central theoretical, methodological, and data-analytic concerns in studying
attrition.

The consortium leaders were aware of the critical role of institutional research in designing an effective strategy for student persistence.
A three-year consortium of eight colleges in California had reported the
general areas in which retention efforts appeared to be effective in their
schools ("Colleges Really Can . . . ," 1984). They lacked a data base, however, that would have permitted them to measure the effect of specific
interventions. We aspired to acquire a baseline of student information
that would enable us to know our students demographically, to target
attrition-prone groups, and to measure students' progress, especially in
the crucial freshman year. Moreover, we intended to obtain information
that would identify the strengths and weaknesses of the various institutional factors—in the academic domain, in administrative policies and
practices, and in student affairs. As a result, we emphasized that the institutional research officer should be a vital member of the retention com-

M. M. Stodt, W. M. Klepper (eds.). *Increasing Retention: Academic and Student Affairs Administrators in Partnership.*
New Directions for Higher Education, no. 60. San Francisco: Jossey-Bass, Winter 1987.

committee on any campus and that any strategy should be developed within a framework for evaluation.

Astin (1975) claims that the major limitation of institutional self-study is the absence of data from comparable institutions that can provide a broad context within which each school can view itself. For this reason we requested that the consortium schools participate in the American Council on Education Cooperative Institutional Research Program (ACE-CIRP), the nation's largest and oldest continuing empirical study of higher education. Their standardized instruments, the Entering Student Survey and the follow-up student questionnaires, offered national norms and a uniform measure for our consortium participants. Some member institutions were already participants in CIRP, and almost all consortium schools subsequently joined the program.

Unfortunately, an insufficient number of our schools were able to modify their institutional research programs rapidly enough for us to present adequate uniform data. Several schools, however, had already launched in-house institutional research, which has begun to provide useful information to the respective institutions. In this chapter, Trenton State College represents an institution that has effectively used the ACE-CIRP instruments for planning and assessment. And the institution-specific research programs of two other institutions, Duquesne University and Canisius College, are presented as illustrations of the vital contribution institutional research can make to educational excellence and retention.

ACE-CIRP and Persistence Predictors

At Trenton State College (and at most consortium schools) the worksheet shown at the conclusion of Astin's *Preventing Students from Dropping Out* (1975) was administered to all first-year students. This information provided a data base on which a forecast of attrition could be made. At Trenton State the college's institutional research office assisted in the design and method for collecting and reporting the data. An optically scored response form was used in order to facilitate the tabulation of results. The responses were grouped into the three categories (white men, white women, blacks) as designated by the worksheet.

The worksheet provides two separate probability scores. The first score is based on the responses to fifty-two of the sixty-four questions. The first group of questions and resulting measurement is a product of the students' demographics and experiences prior to their first year. The second measurement is based on the students' financial aid, work status, and residence during the freshman year. Astin and others have found through their research that these three classes of information add significantly to the prediction of dropout chances (Astin, 1975; Baldridge, Kemerer, and Green, 1982; Beal and Noel, 1980; Forrest, 1982; Hilton,

1982; Hossler, 1984; Lenning, Sauer, and Beal, 1980a, 1980b; Noel, 1978; Pascarella, 1982; and Ramist, 1981).

The students' probabilities of retention gave the schools a realistic range within which they could develop their strategies for reducing attrition. (A realistic range for retention is defined as the existing retention percentage for students at one end of the range and the predicted percentage at the other end of the range.)

For example, the data collected from entering students in fall 1984 at Trenton State College were analyzed using the Astin's worksheet. The analysis revealed that the chances of white women dropping out were 28 percent; white men, 20 percent; and black students, 36 percent. After the factors of financial aid, work, and residence during their freshman year were factored in, the chances of dropping out decreased to 21 percent for white women, 17 percent for white men, and 26 percent for black students.

New Findings on Student Retention Applied to Trenton State College

Astin has recently reported new findings on student retention from the results of the follow-ups of about twelve thousand cases from the 1981 and 1983 entering classes conducted in summer and fall 1985. In his general findings, he states that "retention rates for students in all types of institutions have declined substantially since the early 1970s. By far the important freshman predictors of retention are the students' high school grades and admission test scores" (1987, pp. 38, 39). Comparing the retention rates by type of institution for the class of 1972 and the class of 1985 supports his statement of decline in retention. (See Table 1.)

The decline of approximately ten to thirty percentage points across the six categories of institutions over the thirteen-year period raised the question of the reliability of the probabilities for the 1984–1985 freshmen after four years. Astin has developed a new set of equations that allow institutions to estimate their expected retention rate based on his research

Table 1. Retention Rates by Type of Institution (1968 and 1981 Freshmen)

Received bachelor's degree, completed four years, or still enrolled, by class	*Universities*		*Other Four-Year Institutions*			
	Public (%)	Private (%)	Public (%)	Non-sectarian (%)	Roman Catholic (%)	Protestant (%)
1972	70	79.5	72	74.5	77	70
1985	60.3	70.7	41.4	61	61	50.1

Source: Astin, 1975, 1987.

study of 1981–1982 freshmen after four years (Astin, 1987). Using the new equations, Trenton State College's estimated probability of retention for 1984–1985 majority students would be 58 percent and for minority students, 41 percent.

Trenton State College's institutional research office continues to track the retention rates for the entering class of 1984–1985. Seventy-eight percent of all freshman admits returned after one year, and 66.5 percent returned after two years. For all minority freshman admits, 75 percent returned after one year, and 59 percent returned after two years. The actual retention rates for the entering class of 1984–1985, when set in a range with a fixed floor of the estimated probability of retention, allow the institution to track the students' progress and measure the impact of their efforts. Also, if the rate of return in each succeeding year approaches or goes below the probability rate, the institution can adjust its plan to target those students who are deemed to be at risk of dropping out.

Trenton State College's student development and retention plans included improvement programs in minority student retention and overall student advisement. The freshman attrition for minority students after two years signaled the need to redouble the efforts for increasing their retention. The Minority Executive Council of the college identified the need for a mentoring program to focus on the advisement, orientation, and both the academic and the social environment for the minority student. A full-time coordinator for minority retention will be hired beginning with the 1987–1988 academic year to implement and administer the action steps under each of the program areas.

"In-House" Institutional Research at Duquesne

Duquesne University and Canisius College are two schools in the consortium who maintained the institutional research programs begun prior to the consortium ACE-CIRP effort. If an institution is not in the enviable position of having a sophisticated computerized data collection and software analysis program, the basic trend line data can still be hand collected and analyzed. This effort can produce demographic and descriptive profiles that will assist in identifying and targeting the population for program actions and further research.

Duquesne University's research program provided the foundation and impetus for planning and implementing a comprehensive set of retention actions and programs. It was slow and tedious in its realization, evolving from best estimates of attrition in the late 1970s to more refined and accurate data including pre-enrolled, enrolled, nonreturning, and alumni surveys.

Beginning research on attrition sprang from the Admissions Office during the mid 1970s, when the decline in the birth rate was quite apparent. Admissions officials gathered enough attention to bring in an attrition expert for a symposium in 1978, but the effects of the decline were not felt, and interest diminished. Research plodded on with the hope of converting and convincing the institution of impending danger.

In light of enrollment projections, attrition and graduate rates were collected to investigate the offsetting advantages of retaining those already recruited and enrolled. Transcripts of nonreturning students were collected and analyzed on a semester, annual, and four-to-five-year basis. In the process revenue losses were calculated, which tended to get the attention of the fiscally minded. The analysis of attrition revealed that Duquesne's attrition rate was average but unacceptable because the budget was highly dependent on student-generated revenues. A university-wide retention committee was established at this point, and continued research was mandated.

The analysis of transcripts revealed that 50 percent of those who left over a five-year period were freshmen and 27 percent were sophomores. Approximately 43 percent of those who left had grade point averages (GPA) at or below 2.0. That information instigated the investigation of freshman demographics and the administration of pre-enrollment surveys and marketing surveys. It was established that the freshman cohort constituted one-half of the attrition, but why? Demographics revealed that 84 percent of the entering freshmen ranked in the upper two fifths of their graduating high school class. Because so many of them who did not return had GPAs below 2.0, it was postulated that they had been accustomed to receiving B's or better grades and had entered with high grade expectations. It was also suspected that they had high expectations for a social life as good as or better than their high school experiences. The pre-enrollment survey results supported that speculation. They also provided insight into students' reasons for continuing their education—three of the top six survey items chosen by 94 percent or more pertained to occupational preparation and increasing earning power. Only 30 percent were enrolled in specific career-oriented programs, and only 11 percent of them were in a program where completion would lead to 98 percent placement with a high entering salary.

The preceding information culminated in the hypothesis that freshmen have high academic and social expectations, and that they enter college for a variety of reasons. In admissions and counseling interviews the reasons most students gave for going to college were often general and vague, suggesting that they lacked personal meaning and conviction; for example, "My parents [and I] expected me to," "All my friends went to college," and "To get a better job." While these are legitimate reasons, they lack the clarity of personal goals that provides the motivation, determination, and self-discipline to succeed academically and socially. It appears that many freshmen expect that, simply by attending college, their grades and social life will continue to be as good as or better than they were in high school. This expectation can be realized, but it does not automatically happen; students must do things in new and different ways to make it happen. In summary, many college freshmen seem to unwittingly continue their high school attitudes and behavior in the college environment. Then, when their social and academic expectations are not met, they become dissatisfied and leave. Dissatisfaction with grades and social life were two of the major reasons for dropping out that nonreturning students cited on their surveys.

On the pre-enrollment survey a high percentage of freshmen indicated that they wanted help in speaking, studying, writing, test taking, and math skills. High percentages also indicated an interest in participating in a variety of extracurricular activities. A check with the departments involved (and a review of enrolled student survey activities) revealed that less than one fourth of them actually followed through. Further, they expected high-quality courses, good grades, many activities, organizations, cultural events, caring personnel, job-oriented classes, and comfortable residence halls. It was interesting that many of their expectations paralleled their dissatisfactions and the reasons given for leaving. It was confounding that most of what they wanted and expected was available, but the connections were not being made. As a result of this institutional research, it was decided that it is necessary to help students clarify their expectations, teach them how to make the connections, and demonstrate how they can be more effective in attaining them. The pre-enrollment survey results led specifically to the development of the New Student Seminar, which was designed to assist the freshmen in the transitional process. Most of the course objectives were derived from the research to assist the students in making connections and adjustments.

Surveys of enrolled students and nonreturning students were administered for several years before actions began. It was a prudent decision because the changes implied by the results necessitated profound revisions and resources. Enrolled student research surveys uncovered varying degrees of dissatisfaction with parking, recreational facilities, teaching, advising, and student-faculty and staff interactions. Fortified with this information, the university began to plan retention actions and programs. Construction began on a new parking garage and a new student convocation-recreation center. A centralized Academic Advising and Career Center for freshmen and undeclared upperclassmen is being renovated and staffed. The universitywide Student Opinion of Teaching Effectiveness Survey has been developed and administered in every undergraduate class. All graduate classes will be added.

The process of institutional research and planning began three years ago. For much of that time it appeared as though nothing was happening and probably never would. A word to researcher and retention coordinators—as William Randolph Hearst said, "Tell them what you're going to tell them, tell them, then tell them what you told them." Add to that repetition, persistence, and perseverance ad nauseam, utilizing any and all modes of communication to create awareness and participation, and positive effects will eventually occur.

The institutional research on intra-student processes (student satisfaction and expectations) and on institutional characteristics (via the ratings of academic areas, administrative policies, and student life on campus) added credibility and objective data confirming suspected strengths and deficiencies, enabling the university to act on them. Positive action occurs more quickly if research results emphasize strengths and administrators reward those responsible for progress.

Retention Strategies

Most of the retention programs that Duquesne has initiated have received their impetus directly from the institutional research material. The summary of retention programs and actions that follow constitute the initiation of a comprehensive retention program—an effort to continually improve and monitor the quality of all academic and student support services:

- Universitywide committee on retention with individual school committees who establish attrition reduction goals and are responsible for developing, implementing, monitoring, and evaluating retention programs—actions to enhance the quality of all facets of the students' educational experience
- Continued survey research with students prior to enrollment, during enrollment, on leaving, and at graduation—continued accurate tracking with an attempt to systematically computerize and interface all data for more comprehensive analysis including prediction of attrition
- New Student Seminar—currently in its third year on a voluntary basis (a complete description of this program is presented in Chapter Four)
- Centralization of academic and career advisement with an outreach effort concentrated on all freshmen, undecided-major sophomores, and all students with GPAs below 2.0
- Development of placement testing for English, math, and modern languages
- Student evaluation of teaching effectiveness in every undergraduate course—to be used for developmental programs and consideration in tenure, promotion, and salary increments.

The impact of these efforts cannot be evaluated as yet, but means for assessment are in place.

At Canisius College retention patterns have been studied for much of the past decade. Several modest, preliminary studies contributed to the design and development of intervention programs, and several projects have compared data about students who have left the institution with data on those who stayed. At the same time, the college has been systematically collecting information from students who drop out in an effort to better understand the causes of attrition.

Those early and continuing efforts have led to some understanding about attrition, but the key current research effort is dedicated to predicting risk of attrition in advance. The two key elements of that research are the college student data base and a new study about entering students' characteristics.

College Student Data Base

In 1980 Canisius College began the sizable project of writing the software for its own student data base. That was a long and occasionally painful process, but it has proven its value in retention analysis. From the beginning point of 1982, cohort analyses were easily available, and enrollment tracking has become relatively simple. The data base is the most important resource available to the college for the purpose of retention analysis.

The data base was designed by a team of computer experts, student records experts, academic personnel, and student affairs officials. Its scope represents the wide range of interests the college has in record keeping and student experience tracking. It includes a full range of demographic variables describing a student's background. High school academic performance (and previous college academic performance for transfer students) is recorded thoroughly, as are results from standardized tests. Information about a student's academic program and performance are thoroughly recorded. There are also fields on the data base that describe student experience outside of the classroom. Such fields include student organization participation, athletic team memberships, student employment, honors, and awards. Whether a student attended orientation is on the data base as is the student's assignment to the College Mentoring Program, a program described in a next chapter. This data base forms the core information for the retention analysis currently underway at Canisius College.

Attrition Risk

The most important research project underway at Canisius, particularly relative to retention, is a comprehensive longitudinal analysis that endeavors to generate an attrition-risk formula to be applied to all incoming students and, periodically, to upperclass continuing students. The three analytic groupings for that analysis are persisters, stopouts (those who dropped out and later re-enrolled), and dropouts. Multiple discriminant analysis, with membership in one of these three groupings as the dependent variable will be used to identify which variables tend to discriminate most effectively between the groups. The analysis will specify the form of an attrition-risk equation. The variables in use are comprehensive, combining those from the student data base and those generated by a survey instrument administered to all students at their first entry into the college.

Variables from the student data base include information on demographics, academic performance, academic experience, intake performance (such as high school grade average, rank, and SAT or ACT scores), resident status, registration dates, and participation in programs and activities such as orientation, mentoring, and student organizations. Full financial aid profile information is also part of the system.

Although the existing registration and admissions student data base is sophisticated and very appropriate for other institutional needs, it is not completely sufficient for a comprehensive retention analysis. Therefore, a survey was designed to provide data to supplement that available from the computer data base. The survey is administered to all first-time, full-time Canisius College students, including transfers. Variables on the survey instrument include demographic information not available through the data base, such as parents' level of education. There is also information about amount of time the student expects to work off campus and on campus, the amount of time the student expects to study outside of class, the student's concern for financing his or her education, and the student's impressions of the quality of education at Canisius College. Each of these last four variables has also been added to the student data base of the registration system, so they can be systematically updated every semester. This last condition reflects the flexibility and value of the institutionally designed data base. The survey also covers information about students' reasons for ranking Canisius College as their first choice.

On the survey, the student reflects opinions about social issues, academic abilities and motivations, and personal abilities. Another section of the survey is devoted to values. An additional part of the survey gives students the opportunity to make predictive statements about their own college experiences. A final section addresses the student's high school experiences relative to academic and social matters. Each of the last three sections of the survey borrows heavily from the Cooperative Institutional Research Program (CIRP).

The student data base information has been available since 1982, and the survey was first administered in 1985. After enrollments are tracked over a five-year period, we anticipate that multiple discriminant analysis will provide an attrition-risk formula that will be systematically applied to all incoming students. The college plans to assign a risk-of-attrition score to each incoming student. Those students with particularly high risk scores will, after analysis of the risk sources, be afforded special treatment to include counseling, academic remediation, and financial aid.

Attrition-risk scores will be recalculated each semester, with the formula being updated with changing student academic performance, views, and experience information. This project is a collaboration between academic and student affairs personnel. The project administrators are the dean of students and a faculty member in the School of Business. The Academic Affairs Office is a cosponsor of the project and a source of funding for much project activity.

Conclusion

In our judgment the institutional research office is critically important in developing strategies to improve educational excellence and student retention. Although the consortium was unable to present consortium-wide empirical evidence of the effects of our tactics, the members who followed the CIRP program or systematic research programs of their own have already acquired information that greatly enhances their ability to plan effectively—as illustrated by the foregoing case studies. Furthermore, it seems safe to say that every member institution now has a more organized, cohesive institutional research program due to the consortium's efforts—or at least each member now recognizes the necessity for such.

Scrutiny of the research findings offers clear support for the premise that both the academic and the student affairs domains must be utilized to provide educational excellence and promote student persistence.

References

Astin, A. W. *Preventing Students from Dropping Out.* San Francisco: Jossey-Bass, 1975.

Astin, A. W. "The American Freshman Two and Four Year After Entry." Unpublished manuscript, Higher Education Research Institute, University of California, Los Angeles, 1987.

Baldridge, J. V., Kemerer, F. R., and Green, K. C. "Enrollment in the Eighties: Factors, Actors, and Impacts." *American Association for Education—Educational Resources Information Center/Higher Education Research Report, No. 3.* Washington, D.C.: American Association for Higher Education, 1982.

Beal, P. E., and Noel, L. *What Works in Student Retention.* Iowa City, Iowa: American College Testing Program and National Center for Higher Education Management Systems, 1980.

"Colleges Really Can Cut Their Dropout Rates, Researchers Say." *UCLA News,* no. 216, April 27, 1984.

Forrest, A. *Increasing Student Competence and Persistence: The Best Case for General Education.* Iowa City, Iowa: American College Testing Program and National Center for Higher Education Management Systems, 1982.

Hilton, T. L. *Persistence in Higher Education.* New York: College Entrance Examination Board, 1982.

Hossler, D. *Enrollment Management: An Integrated Approach.* New York: College Entrance Examination Board, 1984.

Lenning, O. T., Sauer, K., and Beal, P. E. *Retention and Attrition: Evidence for Action and Research.* Boulder, Colo.: National Center for Higher Education Management Systems, 1980a.

Lenning, O. T., Sauer, K., and Beal, P. E. *Student Retention Strategies.* AAHE-ERIC/Higher Education Research Report no. 8. Washington, D.C.: American Association for Higher Education, 1980b.

Noel, L. (ed.). *Reducing the Dropout Rate.* New Directions for Student Services, no. 3. San Francisco: Jossey-Bass, 1978.

Pascarella, E. T. (ed.). *Studying Student Attrition.* New Directions for Institutional Research, no. 36. San Francisco: Jossey-Bass, 1982.

Ramist, L. "College Student Attrition and Retention." *College Board Report No. 81-1.* New York: College Entrance Examination Board, 1981.

William M. Klepper is dean of student life at Trenton State College.

John E. Nelson is assistant vice-president of student life and retention at Duquesne University.

Thomas E. Miller is dean of students at Canisius College.

The freshman year offers the greatest opportunity for controlling attrition.

Exemplary Retention Strategies for the Freshman Year

Linda Dunphy, Thomas E. Miller, Tina Woodruff, John E. Nelson

The significance of the freshman year for a successful college experience is not a new idea in higher education. The Committee on the Student in Higher Education, established by the Hazen Foundation (1968), worked for eighteen months on recommendations to improve the college experience, both for students and for society. Their conclusions emphasized the importance of the freshman year and urged colleges to make a major investment in the student's initial year—not for the purpose of retention but in order to foster learning and development. Sixteen years later the National Institute of Education's (1984) report, *Involvement in Learning: Realizing the Potential of American Higher Education,* advocated as its first recommendation the "front loading'" of resources for first- and second-year students in order to increase student learning and encourage persistence. Concomitantly, retention research shows consistently that the highest amount of attrition occurs around the freshman year, either during or just after it.

In accordance with this perspective, the consortium schools

M. M. Stodt, W. M. Klepper (eds.). *Increasing Retention: Academic and Student Affairs Administrators in Partnership.*
New Directions for Higher Education, no. 60. San Francisco: Jossey-Bass, Winter 1987.

focused immediately on developing freshman-year programs—or nurturing existing ones—that were intentionally designed to support students in their academic and social development and to involve them more deeply with the educational process. Nowhere in the higher education setting is the value of collaboration between academic and student affairs more apparent. In this chapter descriptions of several effective programs are offered.

Trenton State College has a ten-year history of requiring that a college seminar, which is a credited course, be taken by its first-year students. The course's history can be traced from its beginnings as a survival-skills seminar for high-risk students to a general orientation course, and finally to a critical-thinking seminar. An added value of this program is the finding that frequent absences from the course can easily serve as an early warning of likely attrition.

Canisius College has had for over six academic years its Mentoring Program that has proven to enhance student retention and academic performance. The original design of the program and how it has evolved as a program that fosters good will and strong and early bonding to the college is reported later in this chapter.

Rider College has implemented its Academic Intervention Program, which is a group-counseling outreach program developed to assist the academic underachiever to improve academic performance through increased personal awareness. The program has been used successfully with students who entered the college with conditional admittance. This chapter describes the five sequenced phases designed to raise the student's semester grade point average above 2.0 during the semester of treatment.

Duquesne University has been successful in implementing its New Student Seminar, modeled after the universally popular University 101 Program, "The Student in the University," at the University of South Carolina. The history of the development and implementation of a successful extended orientation course is presented.

College Seminar at Trenton State College
Linda Dunphy

Although the aim of student retention has remained the same, the design of the College Seminar Program at Trenton State College has evolved through at least three distinct stages and is on the brink of another. The purpose of this section is to describe each of these stages as well as the internal and external factors that influenced them.

Stage 1: Survival-Skills Seminar. As a response to the high attrition rate of underprepared minority students, the Survival-Skills Seminar and the Basic-Skills Program were begun in 1976 for high-risk students. A summer testing program had revealed that these students were deficient in the areas of mathematics, reading, and writing, and a dual-focus program was devised to help them survive at college. The first focus was academic and consisted of basic-skills coursework in the area in which help was needed. The second focus was on acquainting students with the basics of the campus culture, an acquaintance that any student needs in order to survive (for example, registration procedures, course selection, and study skills). This second focus was in the form of a course, the Survival Skills Seminar, which was taught by an academic adviser and carried one credit. This structured course approach has since become a common strategy in colleges and universities in order to increase student satisfaction and thereby reduce attrition (Eddy, Cochran, and Haney, 1980).

The dual-focus intervention was evaluated after three semesters; the academically deficient students who had participated in the program were compared with students with the same deficiencies who had not participated in the program. Students had been randomly assigned to treatment and nontreatment groups. Participants in the program achieved higher grade point averages (2.30 versus 2.16) and a lower attrition rate (24 percent versus 30 percent) than those students who had not participated in the program.

Stage 2: Freshman Seminar. With increasing documentation of the role of nonintellectual factors in student attrition and the necessity for a "personal touch" (Astin, 1975; Friendly, 1985), college administrators, student affairs professionals, and faculty members began to see a seminar such as this as a useful way to reduce student attrition through intensive advisement. As a result, the Academic Policies Committee made the College Seminar a graduation requirement for all entering full-time, first-time freshmen in 1977.

All parts of the college community were involved in the College Seminar Program during this initial stage of campuswide implementation. The seminar program was headed by the director of the Center for Personal and Academic Development, a psychologist within the Student Affairs Office, and the seminars were taught by volunteers from the faculty, professional staff, and administration. Students who had selected a major were taught by faculty members within their chosen discipline, while students with undeclared majors were taught by a variety of professionals, including the provost, the president, and the assistant dean of students.

With large-scale campus implementation came the necessity for increasing structure: faculty training, student evaluations, standardized curriculum, and an advisory board. Two-day training workshops covered basic campus information so that faculty members would not only be familiar with current policies and services but would be aware of some of the developmental issues confronting students in college for the first time. It soon became clear that college seminar training was serving the function of adviser training. Several faculty members commented that the training would be beneficial for entering faculty members as well as entering students.

Student and faculty evaluations were collected, and they were generally positive, indicating that students had gained an understanding of the college and of their departments. Most students and faculty members also felt that the seminar should continue as a required course for all entering freshmen.

Originally, it was believed that the faculty would not only serve as advisers but that they would also be persons to whom students could turn for help with personal problems related to college adjustment. The early evaluations indicated that this was not the case. Students have different expectations of different campus help providers, and the pattern reported by Tinsley, Brown, de St. Aubin, and Lucek (1984) was also seen at Trenton State College; that is, students turn to advisers for academic and career concerns, not for personal concerns. Since many faculty advisers have neither the interest nor the skills to serve as counselors, the students' perceptions were probably accurate. In any case, referrals to the Counseling Center were encouraged.

The early decision to have the College Seminar carry academic credit and be taught primarily by faculty members rather than student affairs professionals had both costs and benefits. A cost was that most faculty members saw their role as one that fosters a student's intellectual development rather than a student's moral, social, or career development (Miller and Prince, 1976). A benefit was that the course was fully embraced and "owned" by faculty members, who then took responsibility for orienting their own freshmen.

A standardized course outline was distributed during training, and faculty members were encouraged to cover certain key topics. The College Seminar was scheduled to meet once a week for fifty minutes during the first ten weeks of the semester, and faculty members were asked to spend at least one class session on each of the following areas:

- Preregistration procedures and deadlines
- Academic regulations (for example, course withdrawals, grade point averages, dismissals)
- Liberal studies curriculum requirements
- Student life (such as clubs, student services, disciplinary and appeal procedures)
- Test-taking and study skills
- Information about the major (courses required, honors study, tracks, faculty, career options)
- Library orientation.

An advisory board was formed of interested faculty members as well as the Registrar staff, and this group met with the director at least once a year in order to review student evaluations and consider changes of direction for the coming year. The members of the Advisory Board were supportive of the concept of the seminar and had themselves volunteered to teach.

Stage 3: College Seminar. Like most innovations that become incorporated into an organizational structure, the College Seminar came to resemble existing courses within the next five years (1980–1985). Administrative responsibility moved from the Student Affairs Office to the Academic Affairs Office, class size climbed from an average of ten to an average of twenty students per class, instructors were assigned rather than voluntary, and a standardized text was introduced. The commercially produced text received negative reviews from both faculty and students and was replaced after one year by a less expensive college-based manual that briefly outlined academic policies and liberal study course requirements. This manual was supplemented by a student handbook that described student activities as well as disciplinary and appeals procedures.

With increasing student and parental interest in careers, and the increasing assumption by colleges of a role in educational advisement and career planning (Shipton and Steltenpohl, 1981) three of the ten class sessions for students with undeclared majors were devoted to career exploration. About ten of the fifty College Seminar classes were composed of such students; these classes were taught by professional staff members with career-counseling backgrounds, and students were encouraged to use computerized career exploration inventories in order to identify a tentative major. The DISCOVER System, available to students in the Office of Career Planning and Placement, was an aid in career exploration as well as a source of up-to-date labor demand and salary projections for a variety of careers.

Although student and faculty evaluations of the College Seminar had been consistently positive, more sophisticated analyses of the effects of the College Seminar became possible in 1984 with the advent of a computerized student data base. The initial assumption that the College Seminar would lead to increased student retention was examined by reviewing longitudinal data from first-time, full-time freshmen who entered the college in fall 1978, 1979, 1980, 1981, 1982, and 1983. For purposes of analyzing the effect of the College Seminar, students were separated into two categories: *regular admits*, the bulk of the students who met regular admission criteria, and *special admits*, students who did not meet the usual admission criteria but who were admitted for reasons of cultural diversity (for example, Educational Opportunity Fund students, students with athletic or artistic talents). The regularly admitted students who entered in the fall of each of the six years were then divided into three groups: those who passed the College Seminar (n = 5334), those who failed the College

Seminar (n = 218), and those who, through some hole in the administrative net, did not take College Seminar at all (n = 113).

Once it had been determined who had taken the College Seminar and who had not, it was possible to see if there were differences among the groups regarding retention. *Retention* is defined as that category of successful students who are either currently enrolled, with grade point averages of 2.0 or higher, or students who have graduated from the college. *Attrition* is defined as that category of unsuccessful students who left the college with grade point averages less than 2.0. Students who passed the College Seminar had a higher retention rate (65.3 percent) than either those who did not take College Seminar (42.5 percent) or those who failed it (12.4 percent). These differences are significant at the .01 level (chi square 271.4, *df* = 2) and are reflected in Table 1.

It can be seen from Table 1 that the majority (94 percent) of the entering freshmen took and passed the College Seminar; however the small percentage of students who did not take it or who failed it had a considerably higher rate of attrition. In viewing the percentages it must be kept in mind that they do not reflect a sample but an actual population; that is, all of those regularly admitted students who came to the college in the fall during the years 1978 through 1983. Although the percentage of students who either failed or did not take the College Seminar and subsequently left is small, it represents 256 students who could have been retained.

The students who failed or did not take the College Seminar were not appreciably different from those who passed at the time of entry: Their high school ranks, SAT scores, and predicted grade point averages were similar (Table 2). Differences between the groups emerged only after they arrived, when their grade point averages began to diverge and they began to leave the college. The students who failed the College Seminar were the ones who fared worst: 78 percent of them left, with a mean grade point average of 1.36. These students experienced a decisional crisis of some kind but could not be reached by the faculty or other students in their College Seminar because they chose not to attend, nonattendance being the most common reason for seminar failure. Given that most student attrition occurs during the first few weeks of the first semester, it is likely that the lower grade point average of these students reflects an early decision not to commit themselves to the college. Once this decision has been made, attendance at an orientation course no longer makes sense. Nonattendance in such a course could easily serve as an early warning of likely attrition.

Changing state regulations concerning the preparation of teachers led to drastic curriculum revision and the elimination of the College Seminar as a graduation requirement for education majors, beginning in 1984. Faculty members within the School of Education continued to meet

Table 1. Relation Between College Seminar Performance and Percentage of Attrition

| | College Seminar Status of Students 1978–1983 | | |
	Failed	Did Not Take	Passed
Academic Attrition	87.6	57.5	34.7
	(n=191)	(n=65)	(n=1851)
Retention	12.4	42.5	65.3
	(n=27)	(n=48)	(n=3483)

Table 2. Description of Students Who Failed, Did Not Take, or Passed the College Seminar 1978–1983

	Failed	Did Not Take	Passed
Mean High School Rank	71	73	77
Mean SAT	949	944	941
Mean P.G.P.A.[a]	2.56	2.62	2.65
Mean G.P.A.	1.36	2.27	2.66

[a]A student's predicted grade point average (PGPA) is obtained by differentially weighting the student's high school rank, SAT-verbal, SAT-Math, and an admission officer's evaluation.

their entering freshmen for group advisement in many departments, however, despite the fact that credit was no longer awarded.

Stage 4: The Present College Seminar. A number of national reports, including *Involvement in Learning* (National Institute of Education, 1984), the report of the Study Group on Conditions of Excellence in American Higher Education, began to emphasize the importance of personal contact between students and faculty on intellectual issues as well as the importance of a systematic program of student advisement.

Accordingly, the College Seminar classes composed of students with undeclared majors were identified as a pilot group with which to focus on intellectual issues as well as advisement information. The advisement information is currently covered for this pilot group in large workshops and videotapes, and students have the opportunity to test this segment of the course. Smaller groups of students with undeclared majors meet with faculty volunteers from the School of Arts and Sciences for forty minutes, twice a week, for the first ten weeks of the semester. In these small groups faculty members focus on particular liberal arts topics, ranging from "The Science Fiction Novel" to "The Politics of the Third World and South America," and students are required to write a paper by the end of the seminar.

This shift in a portion of the content of the College Seminar reflects not only national trends but also a changing type of student entering the college. Rising SAT scores have placed the college in the "very competitive" admission range (*Barron's Profiles of American Colleges,* 1986), and most first-year students are recent high school graduates and live in residence halls. A seminar format focusing on thinking and writing in a small group with an experienced liberal arts professor may be an ideal way to foster student involvement and retention.

To summarize the stages of the College Seminar at Trenton State College within the last ten years is, in a sense, to summarize stages in the development of the college itself as well as national changes in both student demographics and expectations of higher education. The College Seminar has evolved from a small, focused program for basic-skills students to a general orientation course, to a critical-thinking seminar.

What has remained constant is a continuing awareness of changing student needs and a commitment to the centrality of a faculty role in advisement and orientation. A college seminar program taught by the faculty, with an academic style, can serve the purpose of a goal frequently espoused (Miller and Prince, 1976; Garland, 1985) by involving the faculty in student development. Thus far, this hybrid of student affairs goals and academic affairs style has worked rather well at Trenton State College.

The Mentoring Program at Canisius College
Thomas E. Miller

Canisius College is a small liberal arts institution with a student population that is largely composed of commuters. Only about 20 percent of the full-time, undergraduate population lives in college residences. The college is committed to the personalization of services to students and to conveying the natural warmth and sense of community that exists within the college atmosphere. These factors led to the possibility of a very broad approach to improving retention, and in that environment the Mentoring Program was designed.

Although sincere care for individual students and concern for their welfare is clearly felt by those within the college community, some students did not have the opportunity to benefit from or even notice that care. They were "falling through the cracks" and not receiving the personalized care that the college espoused. The Mentoring Program was designed to provide systematic attention to this matter. It was intended to enhance the relationships of new students with faculty members and administrators and with each other. The specific objectives of the program were:

- To arrange for senior faculty and staff members of the college community to have a positive impact on new students, so that their assimilation into the academic community is aided

- To provide a support group of peers for new students, so issues of mutual concern could be addressed in a peer-group setting
- To personalize the academic environment for new students
- To enhance relationships between new students and faculty members and administrators
- To provide a continuing orientation to college life and increase the involvement of new students in the academic community
- To aid new students in developing the skills necessary for them to cope with their challenges and improve their chances for academic success
- To help students identify positively with the college by conveying concern for and care to them.

Program Administration and Origins. Mentors were recruited from all segments of the faculty and administration. All academic disciplines and administrative sections of the college were represented. Mentoring was voluntary, and mentors were not compensated for their participation. The original collection of mentors experienced a series of training sessions during the summer of 1980. During those sessions they were briefed on the goals and expectations of the program, and they were provided with support material to help them in their task. Various techniques and exercises were described, and mentors were encouraged to supplement those ideas with some of their own.

The original design of the Mentoring Program was a simple scientific method. One half of the new students entering in fall 1980 were randomly chosen for inclusion in the Mentoring Program. The mentoring groups met for the first time during the orientation period. They were typically groups of seven or eight new students, the mentor, and an upperclass student assigned to assist in the guidance of the discussion and to supplement observations of the mentor or the students. The typical mentoring group met four more times during the fall semester and twice during the spring semester. An agenda was prepared for each specific group meeting, designed to meet the students' needs in a timely fashion. For example, study-skills and goal-setting exercises were used in the beginning of the first semester, time management was the agenda as midterm examinations approached, and stress management was covered before finals began.

The goals of the program were clearly outlined to each mentor, but mentors were encouraged to independently design experiences for students that they felt were most appropriate for their individual groups.

Results. Several evaluative techniques were used to monitor the impact of the program. Since half of the new student population was in the Mentoring Program and half was not, simple contrasts between these two groups provided useful information about the impact of the program.

The college engages in an early warning system whereby students who are in danger of failing courses receive midsemester notification, "deficiency notices," that their performance is unsatisfactory. A comparison of the deficiency notices received by students in the Mentoring Program with those not in the program showed a dramatic difference. Of the students not in the program 39.1 percent received deficiency notices, while only 17.7 percent of the mentored students received such notices.

At the end of the first semester, academic performance of the two groups was studied. Students in the Mentoring Program had an almost 50 percent lesser likelihood of attaining a grade point average below 2.0. The most important contrast, in many ways, came from an analysis of students who left the institution. Nonmentored students dropped out from Canisius at a rate consistent with the first semester attrition figures for the previous four or five years (10.6 percent). However, students from the Mentoring Program dropped out at a much lower rate (2.7 percent). This figure alone secured the future of the Mentoring Program and almost made further evaluation of the program unnecessary. However, academic performance of the two groups continued to be studied, as did longer-range enrollment patterns. The trends reported earlier continued, although the contrasts were less striking as time went on.

Current Program. In the intervening six academic years, the Mentoring Program has experienced considerable evolution. The exact nature of the various stages of the program is not important, but the current program reflects a satisfactory and effective way of achieving the original goals of the Mentoring Program in an efficient manner.

Two contrasts should be drawn between the original Mentoring Program and the current one. First, the Mentoring Program no longer focuses on the immediate, primary involvement of the mentor. In the early years of the program, there were several mentoring groups that were disappointing experiences for the mentors or, occasionally, for the new students. At the same time, there were mentoring experiences that were enriching and invigorating exchanges for all involved. Virtually without exception, the mentors who had negative or unpleasant experiences had doubts about the effectiveness of the upperclass student assigned to their groups. And those faculty members who had uplifting experiences gave much of the credit to the upperclass student. It was then decided that the program should begin with a focus on the returning student, the orientation assistant, who introduces the students to the program and coordinates, often alone, the first few meetings. Now only after the group has met with the orientation assistant at least once and often twice does the group meet the mentor. This relaxes the burden on mentors to arrange meetings and accommodate occasionally difficult logistical situations. At the same time, it gives the upperclass student, the one who has typically experienced the program himself or herself, the opportunity to introduce new students to the program and ease them into it.

The second change from the original program is that all students entering the college for the first time in a full-time capacity are included in the program. One of the advantages of this program is that it is entirely systematic. No students are excluded, and it is impossible for a student to escape assignment to a mentoring group. Assignment to a mentoring group means, at a minimum, that the student is contacted by an upperclass student and invited to a meeting to talk about the college, and the student is informed about the existence of a faculty mentor. Attendance at these first mentoring meetings is about 92 percent.

There are a few students who somehow escape assignment to the Mentoring Program in the beginning, such as late enrollees, but even they are identified and assigned to a special group. The suspicion is that those registering latest might be at greatest risk of attrition, so great effort is expended to ensure that no students, and certainly not those who come to the college at the last minute, are missed in this effort to convey the sincere care and concern of the college community about the individual student.

Mentors are regularly informed about the progress of the students in their groups. When deficiency notices are distributed at midsemester, each mentor receives a list of the students receiving such notices. Additionally, at the end of the registration period for the spring semester (usually in early November) mentors are informed about students from their groups who have not registered for classes for the spring.

The results of the Mentoring Program at Canisius College seem quite clear. It is a program that has proven to enhance student retention and academic performance. Evaluations conducted with various participants over the years have shown that it is also a program that fosters good will and commitment to the college. The program provides an opportunity for the college to demonstrate its concern for students. Not all colleges can do that, and this ability of Canisius College is deeply appreciated. A very wide cross-section of the college community has been actively involved in this program, collaborating to ensure its success. The program has enhanced relationships between faculty members and administrators and students.

The Academic Intervention Program
Tina Woodruff

Academic underachievement on the college level is often addressed through the use of study-skills programs. For the student whose underachievement is the result of a weak academic foundation, study-skills programs can be very successful. However, there is a positive correlation between self-esteem problems and weak academic performance. Academic failure is often the result of an emotional dysfunction in response to personal, social, or environmental situations that are beyond the coping capacity of the student. Therefore, for students whose underachievement is tied into emotional conflict and low self-esteem, study-skills programs have not been found to have successful longitudinal results. This may also be the case for some students with a weak academic foundation. The student will continue to fail unless that student's failure identity is intercepted by therapeutic intervention. Academic success or failure, however, is not solely a personal experience. It is played out in the context of a classroom group with an assigned leader. The failure pattern is therefore more effectively intercepted within a context that provides access to both a group and a leader.

The Academic Intervention Program is a group-counseling outreach program developed to assist the academic underachiever to improve academic performance through increased personal awareness. The development of the program was based on the premise that there is a pattern of personality traits common to the academic underachiever. These include a lack of motivation, a fear of failure or success, a fear of taking risks, social insecurity, and a weak, inconsistent value system. The underachiever also exhibits low creative confidence. The program is designed to help underachieving students to identify and overcome the blocks to their success. The program was not originally designed for students admitted to college with known academic deficiencies; rather it was developed for the student with past academic success who is now experiencing academic struggle. However, the program has had some success with students admitted to college conditionally. The program was developed and expanded over a three-year period. Of its 380 participants, 80 percent have raised their semester grade point averages above the 2.0 level during the semester of treatment, as compared to 25 percent of a control population.

The Academic Intervention Program follows five sequenced phases, designed to have an impact on the student for one full semester. Each phase is interrelated and integral to the program's success.

In the first phase, all students with a grade point average below 2.0 receive a letter mailed to arrive at their homes one week prior to the start of a new semester. The letter is written in an authoritative tone, announcing that the student, who has been placed on conditional academic standing, is eligible to participate in the Academic Intervention Program. The letter is intentionally filled with pressure statements alluding the potential of dismissal from college. It is crucial to arouse concern in the underachiever to motivate him or her to attempt change. These students are afraid of taking risks; therefore they must feel an external pressure to follow through on the letter's invitation to attend a meeting during the first week of the upcoming semester to find out more about the program. Reminder notes are sent to the students through the campus mail, and these are timed to arrive two days prior to the scheduled meeting.

During the second phase the evening orientation meeting is held the first week of the semester, at which time the program director presents the purpose of the program and outlines the commitment requirements and a brief overview of what the students will experience. The authoritative tone present in the letter is now replaced by a caring, understanding attitude. A major theme at the meeting is the sense of control and power that each student has over his or her own success. Participation in the program is presented as a choice that the student can make. It is during this phase that the students are given the chance to take a first step toward their own academic success. The goal is to have the student feel proud of the choice. The option to choose not to participate is present. Confidentiality is a rule of participation. All interested students sign up for an intake interview scheduled with a group leader, to take place over the following two weeks.

The third phase is the intake interview, which is a brief individual session with a counselor who will serve as one of the group leaders. The student discusses his or her past semester deficiencies, both on an academic and on a personal level. The counselor is warm and supportive. The student is informed of the requirements for participation: mandatory attendance at every group session and respect for the confidentiality of each group session. The intake interview more subtly removes the anonymity that so often contributes to underachievement. The student is notified within one week of his or her group assignment and schedule.

In phase four the students participate in eight weekly, one-hour group meetings. The exercises and activities are thematic and sequential, designed to lead the student through levels of self-exploration. The weekly themes integrate self-awareness and achievement awareness. The leader's role is crucial to the program's success. Having gone through a training program, the leader-counselor understands the basic needs of the group as it advances through the various stages of development.

Session one is designed to introduce the students to the basic elements of a successful group. Rules are established, and the leader's expectations are presented. Through the exercises in this session, the students understand that everyone in the group has similarities; no one is alone in the desire to survive academically at college. The focus is on simultaneously enhancing group and individual confidence. The student begins to identify as a group member and feel trust in the leader.

The exercises for sessions two and three focus on having the participants begin to identify with student roles and stressors that influence competency, both academically and socially. The focus is on the participants' understanding of who they are as students and what is behind how they behave. The students are taught the differences between cognitive and affective behavior. Discussion and role playing contribute to their understanding of how these two modes can affect a situation's success or failure. For example, a classroom environment requires operation on a cognitive level; however, if a student is responding only on an affective level, the behavior may be inappropriate and could inhibit learning. A goal of these two sessions is to have the students begin to observe the similarities between their academic and social behaviors. As a freshman, social and academic roles are intertwined. It is important for the students to understand that failure in one role can effect failure in the other. Conversely, success in one can transfer to the other.

Session four looks at the influence of the home environment through a focus on birth order and family history. A series of role-playing exercises demonstrate how we have all learned to survive events over which we have little control. Within the program, over 60 percent of the participants have experienced either a divorce or a death of someone significant within the past ten years. The exercises help the group observe the effect stress has on a family and how that can influence their behavior. Session four is a turning point. Previous sessions focus on more externally oriented situations. At this point, the students begin to look inward for explanations of behavior and attitudes.

The fifth session is individually oriented, with each student working independently within the group on a lifeline analysis of how personal experiences have affected achievement. It is a chance for students to look analytically at past successes as well as failures. It is crucial for the students to discover a pattern to their past behavior. Understanding successful behavior is as important as understanding underachievement. The leader is a facilitator, moving through the group, giving each student individual contact and assisting with perceptual insights. Traditionally, the emotional level is very high during this session.

Session six is designed to get the students to think about the future, beyond the college years. The group members complete a career exploration exercise that helps them focus on personality traits, values, and realities of the professional world. For many, this is the first opportunity to look at what is involved in a career decision and how the college years function in relationship to their future.

The seventh session is the final working session. It is structured as a wrap-up. It provides an opportunity to link a common purpose to the outcome of the experiences of the previous sessions. Through an affectively oriented exercise, students share personal insights about themselves and bond as a group.

Session eight is a celebration.

The success of the group sessions goes beyond the actual exercises. There is a balance in the dynamics between a traditional counseling group and a traditional classroom group. The sessions are held in classrooms to facilitate comfort in the environment where the student has experienced the anxiety of failure. There is a blend of counseling empathy with a demanding, goal-oriented approach. The students receive homework that is relevant to experiences both inside and outside of the group. The classroom-group dynamic provides a context that permits the transfer of newly acquired, positive student behaviors to the ongoing academic setting.

Each student maintains a written journal that is shared only with the group leader. Following each session, the students have five minutes to react to the meeting by writing down something that is happening in a class or any other thoughts or concerns. The leader responds in writing to the student in the journal, which is returned at the start of the next session. This serves as a safe, confidential vehicle for the student to receive supportive and constructive feedback.

In the end, the student must initiate the change from a failure identity to a success identity. The sessions bring understanding to previous failures, but the student must give himself or herself permission to succeed. When this level is achieved, the student succeeds in classes, which is reported back to the leader in journals, and, ultimately, to the group for celebration.

The fifth phase is the conclusion of the eight group sessions, and each student meets individually with the group leader for a wrap-up session, during which personal reactions to the group experience are discussed, and long-term goals are clarified. A connection has been made between the student and the leader, to be utilized over future semesters. The program is timed to conclude one week prior to final examinations. Traditionally, students will seek out the group leader to share results of exams and to say one last good-bye before the semester ends.

The Academic Intervention Program (see Figure 1) capitalizes on the influence of the peer group and the students' desire for adult support, through the use of group sessions and the development of a positive relationship with the leader. The program provides an environment that promotes honesty in response, motivates the establishment of goals, and initiates a pattern of self-help.

Developing an Extended Orientation Course
John E. Nelson

Beginning an orientation course can be quite a challenge. Decisions have to made regarding the length of the course, credit or noncredit bearing, grades or pass-fail, course content and objectives, faculty selection and training, whether it is to be voluntary or required, promotion and marketing, and obtaining acceptance and support to actually offer the course.

The first step at Duquesne was to consider the rationale for an orientation course and how to obtain acceptance and support. Faculty

Figure 1. Academic Intervention Program: Model for Group Sessions

	Theme	Affective-Cognitive	Counselor's Role	Group Processes
1.	Who Are We?	Affective Focus Cognitive Wrap-Up	Supportive, Warm Nurturing	Diads
2.	Who Am I (as a student)?	Cognitive Focus Affective Wrap-Up	More Directive Questioning, Supportive	Group as Unit During Role Playing
3.	What Is Behind How I Behave?	Cognitive-Affective Affective Wrap-Up	Directive, Supportive	Group Initiates Confrontation
4.	Accepting, Understanding—Taking Control (part 1)	Affective Focus Affective Wrap-Up	Facilitative	Group Assumes a More Directive Role
	Turning Point		*Turning Point*	*Turning Point*
5.	Accepting, Understanding—Taking Control (part 2)	Affective Focus Cognitive/Affective Wrap-Up	Counselor Role and Group Processes are from this point contingent on the direction taken by the group	
6.	Setting Goals (personal and student)	Cognitive/Affective Affective Wrap-Up		
7.	Being and Becoming	Affective Focus Cognitive Wrap-Up		
8.	Wrap-Up and Celebration			

members sometimes feel that this type of course is not an academic endeavor and object to its being given academic credit (Caple, 1964). However, if the course is noncredited, students question its value and wonder why they should take it. The credit issue seems to swing back and forth. Recently, largely due to attrition and retention concerns, awarding credit is more in vogue (Felker, 1973). The Duquesne course founders supported the credit-bearing course and proceeded to present their ideas to the Council of Academic Deans in March 1983, the Core Curriculum Committee in fall and spring 1984, and the College Curriculum Committee in fall 1984 and spring 1985. The course was ultimately approved in spring 1985 by the College Curriculum Committee for one semester, bearing one credit, and being offered on a voluntary experimental pilot basis.

The Council of Deans turned down the proposal because they felt that it was not needed at Duquesne. The initial proposal highlighted the need for such a course based primarily on the high attrition rate of freshmen. The proposal was modeled on the University 101 Program, "The Student in the University," at the University of South Carolina. This is a three-credit course for twenty to twenty-five freshmen, led by faculty members who have been trained in a forty-hour workshop. Since its inception in 1982, Duquesne had carefully monitored and researched its success, demonstrating that it resulted in higher retention rates, increased student knowledge, and participation in support services and extracurricular activities. At that time some forty other programs had sprung up across the nation based on the University 101 Program.

The second proposal to the Core Curriculum Committee was strengthened by the results of enrolled students' opinions polls and those of nonreturning students that reinforced the value of the course. The Core Curriculum Committee found merit in the proposal but, due to pressures to include other academic units, could not fit it into their program. They also had some moderate reservations about the academic substance of the course.

Finally, the College Curriculum Committee, due in part to additional research results on pre-enrolled freshmen's expectations, approved the course as a one-year pilot with continuance contingent on its merits being demonstrated by research evaluation. The accepted pilot course was offered for one credit, for one semester, on a voluntary basis, with letter grades assigned and one unexcused absence permitted.

Demonstrating the Need for an Extended Orientation Course. The New Student Seminar at Duquesne is a program that emanated and gained support from institutional research. From the analysis of their attrition rates, enrolled and nonreturning student satisfaction or dissatisfaction rating surveys, and pre-enrollment surveys, it was clear that freshmen were encountering difficulty. A freshman study at Pennsylvania State University by James Kelly highlights some findings that had similarities to Duquesne's and may be universally true ("The Great Expectations . . . ," 1985). The study indicated that the 1,144 freshmen entering two-year programs and the 10,000 entering four-year programs had highly unrealistic expectations about their choice of major, grades, study skills, and study hours.

Duquesne found that their freshmen had very high expectations regarding their grades, social life, teaching, activities, organizations, job-oriented courses, cultural events, and caring personnel. The freshmen also expressed a need for assistance in speaking skills, study skills, test taking, and selecting a major. Although resources and programs were available to address their expectations and needs, subsequent research indicated that less than one quarter of the students followed through on their own. While freshman attrition rates provided the impetus to begin the efforts for an extended orientation course, additional research was needed to gain its acceptance. For many years Duquesne students have been conducting an extremely successful five-day, preclass freshman orientation. In fact, it is so successful, rated at 4 on a five-point scale, that the developers of the extended course felt that students might experience a severe social let-down for several weeks after it ends. Inadvertently, that program may have been reinforcing many of the high (unrealistic) expectations. The New Student Seminar evolved as a means of filling the gap and dealing with a multitude of transitional difficulties including clarifying expectations, values, and educational and career objectives; improving social and academic adjustment skills; and increasing interpersonal skills and participation in learning, extracurricular activities, and utilization of helping resources. These objectives were based on student development and emphasized enhancing the students' experiences in college that correlate positively with persistence, including improving grades (Astin, 1975; Pascarella, Duby, Miller, and Rasher, 1981; Bean, 1983), significant relationships with others (Lenning, Sauer, and Beal, 1980; Noel, 1978; Ramist, 1981; Tinto, 1975), involvement in learning and extracurricular activities (Lenning, Sauer, and Beal, 1980), and social interaction (Tinto, 1975; Terenzini, Lorang, and Pascarella, 1981).

The Pilot Course. After demonstrating the need and gaining acceptance for the seminar, founders needed to specify the goals and the specific student development objectives. Five general goals were developed to enhance student adjustment:

1. Acquire a sense of community in the university and better understand its philosophy, objectives, and structure.
2. Begin to identify skills deficiencies and locate and encourage utilization of resources for improvement.
3. Increase awareness of the relationship between education, personal development, and educational and career choices.
4. Identify concerns and work toward their resolution.

5. Improve students' overall college experience and academic performance.

These goals were translated into specific student development objectives that served as the basis for the course content, projects, and assignments:

- Develop a sense of community and social networking
- Develop dialogue and interaction between the faculty and students—limited lecture that is process-oriented to increase involvement in learning
- Provide feedback on study skills, time management, values, goals, career explorations, public speaking, and discovery of resources for further development
- Help students understand the educational objective and philosophy of the university
- Develop a positive attitude to enhance motivation
- Help students understand problem-solving and student support services and campus organizations
- Increase academic performance.

New Student Seminar Sessions. The seminar development staff believed that the process style of the course would be best facilitated by an interactive approach. Thus, classes were limited to fifteen students, all participants sat in a circle, discussion topics were explored in smaller rather than larger discussion groups, and site visits and personal interviews were utilized for information gathering.

The topics for the twelve main sessions for the pilot were (1) interpersonal ice breakers, (2) study skills, (3) oral presentations, (4) common freshman problems, (5) values and careers, (6) time management, (7) faculty/administrators interviews, (8) testing strategies, (9) preparing for research and life, (10) university—organizations, philosophy, goals, (11) library research, and (12) discussion and review. In addition, each student was required to make three entries a week in a journal pertaining to their school activities, but open to other areas. The journals were handed in for the instructor's review. From the faculty point of view, the journals provided insight and early information regarding student difficulties. Faculty members then dealt with the students or referred them to the appropriate center for immediate assistance. Although there were fifteen class sessions, room was intentionally left for discussion and exploration of issues of spontaneous interest to the students. (For additional information on current programs and leaders in the field, contact the National Orientation Directors Association [NODA], refer to Beal and Noel [1980], and read Upcraft's *Orienting Students to College* [1984].)

Faculty Selection. Criteria for the seminar instructors were established early on. The development team felt that it was important for the teachers to be student-oriented, to possess good presentation and interpersonal skills, and to share a strong belief in this type of retention effort. Additional effort was made to include persons who could increase faculty involvement with students; develop enthusiasm, interest, and a cooperative spirit throughout the university; and increase the understanding of student problems and their resolution. The pilot faculty consisted of four faculty members from various departments and schools, an assistant dean of students, and an assistant director of residence life.

Faculty Training and Development. Prior to the course, four faculty members were sent to the National Conference on The Freshman Year Experience, sponsored by the University 101 Program founders at the University of South Carolina.

Prior to the course, all of the instructors were required to attend a one-day training session for which they received a small stipend. They were provided with a course outline, handouts for each session, and tips on how to increase interaction. Experts from health services, learning skills, the library, career planning, counseling/testing, and other areas were present to share their perspectives on new-student transition problems.

During the course, every instructor was required to attend a one-hour-a-week seminar in order to share and review their experiences as well as to plan for future sessions. Each section was visited by one of the developers to observe, reinforce the value of the course, and solicit student input on satisfaction and recommended changes.

Student Recruitment. Personal letters, accompanied by a flyer, were sent to each of the incoming freshmen explaining the rationale and values of the course. The freshman advisers were alerted to the course and asked to encourage students to consider it.

One hundred students enrolled. Of these 47 percent chose to take the course with no prompting, and 53 percent of the pilot group members were from a special, academically at-risk population.

Course Evaluation and Results. A survey instrument was developed to assess the students' perceptions of their gains on twenty-five of the course's objectives. It also contained areas for comments, constructive criticism, and recommended changes. The survey was administered to course participants and a random sample of freshmen who did not participate in the course. A *t*-test for independent samples was used to test the significance of mean differences. The research indicated that, when compared to the nonparticipating freshmen, those students who participated in the New Student Seminar felt that they

- Shared a greater sense of community with fellow students
- Were more comfortable talking to their university professors and were more capable of solving problems
- Better understood the university's structure, educational philosophy, and goals

- Were more familiar with the *where* and *how* to obtain academic and personal help
- Were more knowledgeable about personal public-speaking skills
- Were more positive about their overall experience at the university.

These highlighted differences were statistically significant at greater than a 95 percent level of confidence.

Academic Performance. The predicted first-year grade point average for the participating students was 2.32. They obtained a 2.74 grade point average at the end of the first year. The New Student Seminar participants did in fact academically out-perform the control group in terms of exceeding their predicted grade point average.

Summary. Introducing an extended orientation course requires careful planning. Supporting research is often necessary to gain acceptance for the course. Surveys and student admission interviews are important, helpful methods in determining the objectives for the course. Faculty selection and training are crucial to the course's success. If the course is voluntary, recruitment strategies must be developed. The success of the course cannot be determined without evaluation of its major components, namely, course objective attainment.

References

Astin, A. W. *Preventing Students from Dropping Out.* San Francisco: Jossey-Bass, 1975.

Barron's Profiles of American Colleges. (15th ed.) Woodbury, N.Y.: Barrons Educational Series, 1986.

Beal, P. E., and Noel, L. *What Works in Student Retention.* Iowa City, Iowa: American College Testing Program and National Center for Higher Education Management Systems, 1980.

Bean, J. P. "The Applications of a Model of Turnover in Work Organizations to the Student Attrition Process." *Review of Higher Education,* 1983, *6,* 129-148.

Caple, R. B. "A Rationale for the Orientation Course." *Journal of College Student Personnel,* 1964, *6,* 42-46.

Eddy, J., Cochran, J., and Haney, C. "College Student Retention Studies and Strategies." In J. Eddy, J. Dameron, and D. Borland (eds.), *College Student Personnel Development, Administration, and Counseling.* Washington, D.C.: University Press of America, 1980.

Felker, K. R. "GROW: An Experience for College Freshmen." *Personnel and Guidance Journal,* 1973, *51,* 558-561.

Friendly, J. "Preventing Dropouts: Will Personal Touch Prevent College Dropouts?" *New York Times,* Education Section, November 26, 1985, p. 1.

Garland, P. H. *Serving More Than Students: A Critical Need for College Student Personnel Services.* ASHE-ERIC Higher Education Report No. 7. Washington, D.C.: Association for the Study of Higher Education, 1985.

"The Great Expectations of College Freshmen." *National ON CAMPUS Report,* 1985, *13* (15), 1.

Hazen Foundation. *The Student in Higher Education.* New Haven, Conn.: Hazen Foundation, 1968.

Lenning, O. T., Sauer, K., and Beal, P. E. "Student Retention Strategies." *AAHE-ERIC/Higher Education Research Report No. 8.* Washington, D.C.: American Association for Higher Education, 1980.

Miller, T. K., and Prince, J. S. *The Future of Student Affairs: A Guide to Student Development for Tomorrow's Higher Education.* Jossey-Bass, San Francisco: 1976.

National Institute of Education. *Involvement in Learning: Realizing the Potential of American Education.* Washington, D.C.: U.S. Department of Education, 1984.

Noel, L. (ed.). *Reducing the Dropout Rate.* New Directions for Student Services, no. 3. San Francisco: Jossey-Bass, 1978.

Pascarella, E. T., Duby, P., Miller, V., and Rasher, S. "Preenrollment Variables and Academic Performance as Predictors of Freshman Year Persistence, Early Withdrawal, and Stopout Behavior in an Urban, Nonresidential University." *Research in Higher Education,* 1981, *15,* 329–349.

Ramist, L. "College Student Attrition and Retention." *College Board Report 81-1.* New York: College Entrance Examination Board, 1981.

Shipton, J., and Steltenpohl, E. "Educational Advising and Career Planning: A Life-Cycle Perspective." In A. W. Chickering and Associates, *The Modern American College: Responding to the New Realities of Diverse Students and a Changing Society.* San Francisco: Jossey-Bass, 1981.

Terenzini, P. T., Lorang, W., and Pascarella, E. T. "Predicting Freshman Persistence and Voluntary Dropout Decisions: A Replication." *Research in Higher Education,* 1981, *15,* 109–127.

Tinsley, H., Brown, M., de St. Aubin, T., and Lucek, J. "Relation Between Expectancies for a Helping Relationship and Tendency to Seek Help from a Campus Help Provider." *Journal of Counseling Psychology,* 1984, *31* (2), 149–160.

Tinto, J. V. "Dropout from Higher Education: A Theoretical Synthesis of Recent Research." *Journal of Educational Research,* 1975, *45,* 89–125.

Upcraft, M. L. (ed.). *Orienting Students to College.* New Directions for Student Services, no. 25. San Francisco: Jossey-Bass, 1984.

Linda Dunphy is assistant vice-president for academic affairs at Saint Joseph's University and was formerly assistant to the provost at Trenton State College.

Thomas E. Miller is dean of students at Canisius College.

Tina Woodruff is director of student development services at Rider College.

John E. Nelson is assistant vice-president for student life and retention at Duquesne University.

This chapter describes retention programs for minority students; adult, continuing education students; and commuting students.

Pioneer Programs for Retaining "At-Risk" Students

*Stuart J. Sharkey, Pamela M. Bischoff,
Dorothy Echols, Carol Morrison,
Esther A. Northman, Allison Liebman,
Brent Steele*

The consortium schools were given guidelines for implementation of their student development and retention plans that included the identification of areas, programs, and services for attrition-prone groups that needed improvement. The schools relied on their institutional research and reports (self-study, accreditation, needs assessment); direct feedback from students, faculty, and staff; and their own professional evaluation to identify students who were "at-risk."

The literature gives direction for action to an institution seeking to identify problematic students. The National Center for Higher Education Management Systems (NCHEMS), in its manual for conducting student retention studies, says that "minority students drop out more frequently, but evidence is ambiguous as to why" and "older students tend to drop out of traditional curriculum" (Ewell, 1984, p. 14). Ten years earlier, Chickering's research on commuting versus resident students identified the need to overcome the educational inequities of living off campus (Chickering, 1974). Furthermore, Hodgkinson reports in his

M. M. Stodt, W. M. Klepper (eds.). *Increasing Retention: Academic and Student Affairs Administrators in Partnership.*
New Directions for Higher Education, no. 60. San Francisco: Jossey-Bass, Winter 1987.

demographic studies that the decline in high school graduates will be steep from now to 1994, with the greatest decline in the eighteen-to-twenty-four-year-old, full-time, white, and middle class students. A major increase in part-time college students, and a decline in full-time students (Hodgkinson, 1985) will continue. A partnership between the academic and student affairs areas is essential if an institution is to retain these at-risk students. This chapter describes exemplary programs that have focused on minority, older, and commuting students and that have resulted in greater retention.

The University of Delaware has steadily increased its black student enrollment during the 1970s. A new five-year plan began in September 1981 that was part of the State of Delaware's agreement with the Office for Civil Rights to eliminate vestiges of de jure segregation within its public higher education system. The university had recognized that there was a disparity between the retention of white and black students. This chapter describes the steps taken to rectify the situation and move closer to its goal of achieving parity in the retention of black and white undergraduates.

Ramapo State College, in New Jersey, has a majority of its black and Hispanic students enrolled in its Educational Opportunity Program (EOP). This program offers financial aid and a variety of academic support services for students who are economically deprived and educationally underprepared. By definition, these students are "at risk," given their less advantageous secondary school experiences and their poverty. The college's Minority Achievement Program, which links the EOP students in their sophomore and junior year to the Cooperative Education Program, and its outcomes are presented.

Canisius College's Division of Continuing Studies enrolls adult learners in the evening program, a majority of whom hold full-time jobs, are pursuing business majors, and have had some prior higher education. These students are considered "high risk" because of the usual pressures of job, home, and school responsibilities. They are further limited by a lack of adequate academic skills. The advisement program for these students, which has resulted in an improvement in retention from 20 percent to 49 percent, is described.

University of Maryland–Baltimore County has piloted the Commuter Peer Assistance Program due to the higher attrition rate among commuting students than resident students. The program builds on peer monitoring as an approach to assist commuting students. The use of commuter assistant as a peer adviser for fifty commuting freshmen randomly chosen from the 1985–86 entering student population is presented. Students in the pilot program had an 8 percent attrition rate after one year as compared to a control-group rate of 28 percent.

Retention Program for Black Students at the University of Delaware
Stuart J. Sharkey

During the 1970s the University of Delaware made steady progress toward increasing the enrollment of black students. However, in 1978 the Department of Education's Office for Civil Rights conducted a study that led to citation of the State of Delaware for failing to eliminate vestiges of de jure segregation within its public higher education system, which was in violation of Title VI of the Civil Rights Act of 1964. Consequently, a five-year desegregation plan was negotiated between the State of Delaware and the Office for Civil Rights to meet the requirements of the federal criteria. Included in the plan were the University of Delaware, Delaware State College, Delaware Technical and Community College, and the State of Delaware.

The implementation of the five-year plan began in September 1981. The plan was, in effect, a proactive advancement of higher education in the State of Delaware for blacks. The Delaware State Legislature allocated scholarship funds for black Delaware residents. The university stepped up its recruitment of black students and engaged in numerous other activities to improve the education of black high school students and encourage them to enroll in the University of Delaware.

Concurrently, members in the Division of Student Affairs at the University of Delaware had perceived a need to provide more support to black students. In order to obtain the necessary data to support this contention, the vice-president for student affairs appointed a committee to interview all the black freshmen in 1981. Representatives from various departments ranging from counseling to the Dean of Students Office participated in the program. Each person was assigned five black freshman students to interview. The purpose of the interview was to determine how the students were doing; the type of academic advisement they had received; the need, if any, for further academic support; and the resources they used if they needed assistance. While some students were clearly doing well, others were having difficulties. It was determined that some students were taking too many credit hours, taking too many difficult science and math courses, failing to obtain tutoring, or having difficulty with reading and writing assignments. The committee advised these students where they could obtain assistance, suggested that they revise their academic schedules, and had a follow-up meeting with them later in the year.

At the conclusion of the academic year, a report was presented to the university president. The president of the university was urged to take action to improve the retention of black students. The evidence was clear. The president appointed the associate provost for instruction to assume the responsibility to coordinate all retention activities for undergraduate students, with special attention to black undergraduate students. The associate provost was appointed because it was necessary to obtain the support of the eight colleges who were key to the success of any type of program.

The University of Delaware had recognized that there was a disparity between the retention of white and black students and therefore took steps to rectify this. At the outset, the provost informed each academic dean of the associate provost's appointment and requested their full cooperation. The associate provost met with the vice-president for student affairs and the vice-president for personnel and employee relations, as well as with administrators responsible for facilities and maintenance, and university police. Each person was asked to determine ways in which their units could contribute to improving the academic environment for black undergraduate students. In addition, the Division of Student Affairs was asked to develop programs and services to promote black and white student interaction and contribute to black students' academic and developmental growth.

To assist the associate provost with the task, an all-university advisory committee on the retention of black undergraduate students was appointed. The committee was composed of faculty, academic deans, and representatives from student affairs. The committee met every three weeks during its first year, conferring with black students, faculty, and staff for the purpose of developing university recommendations pertinent to improving the academic environment for black undergraduate students. The following recommendations were made:

1. Each academic dean was to establish a college advisory committee on the retention of black undergraduates. The committee was to include faculty representatives as well as professional staff members who advise the dean on the development and implementation of college policies and procedures pertinent to the retention of black undergraduate students.

2. Each dean was to encourage departments to include relevant materials about black culture in regular curriculum offerings.

3. All departments, in conjunction with assistant and associate deans, were to develop and implement procedures for one-to-one counseling and advising of black undergraduate students each semester on course selection, preference of major, and additional opportunities for educational growth, such as travel study courses, field experience and internships, London and Vienna semesters, Fulbright scholarships, graduate school opportunities, career opportunities, the National Student Exchange, and others. Students who experienced difficulties were to be referred to the appropriate academic support services with follow-up by college personnel.

4. Special advising and counseling was to be conducted for the best and brightest black undergraduate students in the college, and college recognition was to be granted to those students.

5. Teaching assistants were to be informed about college policies and procedures and were urged to work with black students who needed more than usual assistance.

6. Each semester the assistant and associate deans were to review each black student's course selection in conjunction with SAT scores, grade point averages, and predicted grade indexes. If changes in course selection were needed and feasible, students were requested to make an appointment for advisement.

7. Departments were to recommend that black students with appropriate grades be granted the opportunity to become tutors.

8. Faculty members were to develop procedures to ensure that black students who were assigned to student groups for academic work, such as laboratories and group assignments, have a positive environment in which to do their work.

9. Deans were to arrange for the development and implementation of college and departmental workshops on the retention of black students. Reports from these workshops were to be provided for the deans.

Each academic dean was expected to report annually to the Retention Committee about the activities in their college for the preceding year. In the first year, after each of the colleges established advisory committees, they began conducting different activities. For example, they held discussions in faculty meetings on ways to improve the academic environment for black undergraduates, they conducted workshops on issues of concern to black students, they utilized on- and off-campus consultants, and they asked departmental representatives (in some colleges) to develop and maintain counseling procedures. All black undergraduates received one-to-one academic advising.

Some black students resisted coming for advisement, and during the first year, only 87 percent of the black undergraduate students participated in individual advisement sessions. Of the students who were advised to make changes in their registration, 61 percent complied with the advice.

Academic departments were instructed to seek ways of incorporating academic material about black cultures into their courses. The committee recognized that implementation would vary with the academic discipline. The university library compiled bibliographies of available material regarding blacks and black cultures. College teaching assistants were instructed to be prepared to give assistance to black undergraduates. Several colleges established recognition programs for students who had demonstrated excellent academic achievement. One college, the College of Engineering, held an academic recognition banquet for black undergraduates who had maintained excellent academic records. Other colleges developed their own individual ways of recognizing student accomplishments. All the colleges developed an early monitoring system to provide information on academic performance to students in a manner that would assist them in their future academic activities.

University police representatives met several times with the Black Student Advisory Committee to the Vice-President for Student Affairs. One investigator on the police force was assigned the responsibility of initiating formal contacts with black students at the Center for Black Culture. In addition, special sensitivity training sessions were developed for police officers. A program of "ride along," in which black students accompanied university police on their tour of duty, provided an opportunity for sharing information.

The activities of the Retention Committee included looking into recruitment and admissions, financial aid support for black students, an analysis of midterm grades, black student withdrawal, efforts to promote the employment of more black faculty members, course revisions to include relevant material about black cultures, and development of racial awareness training for new faculty members.

Other activities that have helped in the area of retention include the development of the Visiting Minority Scholars Program. A fund was established to match funds with a department to bring black scholars to the university campus. In addition, a Big Brother/Big Sister Program was established. The purpose of the program was to provide black freshmen and transfer students with information about university services by utilizing black students who develop a camaraderie with the freshmen.

The all-university Retention Committee reviewed the reports from each of the colleges, including the Division of Student Affairs, and made recommendations to them for the forthcoming year. The colleges and vice-presidents' offices were to be judged the following year on the degree of action taken on the recommendations.

The following are some examples of actions that received recognition by the Retention Committee: employing a black secretary in the dean's office, employing additional black faculty members, making a concerted effort in black recruitment, increasing the number of black students making the dean's list, increasing the recognition of black students for significant academic achievement, training black student advisers, developing more multicultural courses, presenting a program called "Careers in Business," and involving black alumni in recruitment.

Vice-President for Student Affairs. Under the leadership of the vice-president for student affairs, the Division of Student Affairs, which is composed of the offices of Admissions, Scholarships and Student Financial Aid, Dean of Students, Counseling and Student Development, Career Planning and Placement, Student Health Service, and Housing and Residence Life, has made the recruitment and retention of black students its first priority. Each department head provided the vice-president with goals and objectives to enhance retention of black students. The activities included increased on-campus employment opportunities for black undergraduates, as well as an increase in black professional staff throughout the Division of Student Affairs. The vice-president for student affairs appointed the Black Student Advisory Committee to advise him on black students' issues and concerns. The committee dealt with issues ranging from food service; residence hall policy; police relations; recruitment of minority faculty, staff, and professionals; and subtle racism in the classroom and in courses. For the 1986–87 academic year, the vice-president for student affairs was selected as co-adviser to the Black Student Union and provided impetus to add black students to the Mortar Board Honor Society. The following are specific examples of the programs and services provided by each department to promote the retention of black students.

Dean of Students Office. A needs survey to determine new programming efforts for black students in the Perkins Student Center was developed. Black students were added to the center's advisory boards. Efforts were made to involve more black students in leadership positions in student government. Student government appointed a committee to study racism and develop a position paper. In 1984–85 a black student was selected chair of the student government administrative affairs committee, and in 1986 a black student was elected vice-president of the student government.

The Center for Black Culture expanded its programs for black students to include a greater variety of events, such as a Herbie Hancock concert, a gospel ensemble, a Benjamin Hooks lecture, bus excursions to New York and Philadelphia theaters, a soul food dinner, a lecture by Ramsey Clark, the Black Arts Festival, a Dick Gregory lecture, and the Miss Black Student Union Pageant.

Housing and Residence Life. Housing and residence life developed a survey to evaluate the effectiveness of programming in the residence halls in meeting the needs of black students. The number of black undergraduate staff members was increased. The Dr. Martin Luther King, Jr., Humanities House, a residence for selected black and white students, founded on the principles of Dr. King, was established. Racial awareness training continued to be a major focus for the residence life staff. An increase in black undergraduate staff members has been a high priority. Each residence hall was required to offer at least one racial awareness program per building.

Counseling and Student Development. The Center for Counseling and Student Development offered a number of workshops that provided direct assistance in helping students manage to meet the demands of the university. The stress management workshops and assertiveness-training programs, in particular, have relevance for students who are learning how to adjust to the demands of higher education.

The Counseling Center's contribution to the university's retention effort was demonstrated by the 197 black students (12 percent of all students requesting counseling) who presented specific concerns about dropping out of school, transferring to another institution, or failing academically in the 1985–86 academic year. Follow-up studies from previous years indicated that these efforts have been very effective.

Career Planning and Placement. A staff member was assigned to develop special programs with minority student organizations. Some of these have included the National Black Student Business League, the Society of Black Engineers, and Upward Bound. The office sponsored the Black Minority Corporate Conference. A variety of black students who had graduated from the University of Delaware in different careers were gathered.

Scholarships and Student Financial Aid. The Scholarships and Student Financial Aid Office obtained increased funding for University Merit Scholarships and National Achievement Scholarships for Outstanding Negro Students.

Admissions. Numerous programs were held to attract black students, including a minority weekend for black high school juniors and seniors from the mid-Atlantic region. Personal interviews were conducted with students in the mid-Atlantic region. Special mailings were made to black students in Delaware and the region, encouraging them to participate in a program entitled "An Afternoon for Minority Students." A newsletter describing college was sent to black eighth and ninth graders in Delaware. The university participated in the College Board Student Search mailings to black students. Black alumni were involved in identifying students and engaging in a phone-a-thon. Early financial awards were made to black students. The university also participated in college fairs throughout the mid-Atlantic region, which focused on black students.

Student Health Service. A photography exhibition portraying contributions made by black physicians and nurses was purchased and hung in the Student Health Service. Also purchased was an exhibition depicting the history of black women in the United States for the last one hundred years, which is hung each year in the Student Center.

Conclusion. In February 1987, a comprehensive summary of the university's progress over the five years of the Title VI plan was presented to the state's Title VI Commission. At present, the progress report and supporting documentation are under review in Washington. The university president has made a commitment to continue the university's efforts in the spirit and intent of the plan.

As far as retention is concerned, the university has moved closer to its goal of achieving parity in the retention of black and white undergraduates. Graduation rates for black undergraduates, the most significant evidence of retention, have increased over the past eight years.

Increasing Student Goal-Directedness:
Linking Cooperative Education and the
Educational Opportunity Program
Pamela M. Bischoff, Dorothy Echols, Carol Morrison

Background: EOP and Cooperative Education. In 1968 the State of New Jersey, responding to the social upheavals of the 1960s and to calls for increased access to higher education, created the Educational Opportunity Program (EOP). This program has endured and continues to offer financial aid, as well as a variety of academic support services for students who are both economically deprived and educationally underprepared. Virtually by definition, EOP students are at high risk for academic failure, given their less advantageous secondary school experiences and their poverty. New Jersey's demographic composition is such that a majority of EOP students are either black or Hispanic. Ramapo College, one of New Jersey's public, four-year colleges, currently enrolls 224 EOP students, of whom 173 are members of minority groups. The current full-time student body at Ramapo numbers 1827 students. Since there are only small numbers of non-EOP minority students enrolled at the college, aggressive action to all EOP students must take place if the college is to fulfill its obligations to all New Jersey's citizens and prevent student attrition.

The Cooperative Education Program was initiated at Ramapo College in 1980 and grew rapidly, so that today 25 percent of Ramapo's full-time students gain field placements under its auspices. The program's expansion occurred quickly after a substantial demonstration grant was awarded to Ramapo College by the United States Department of Education in 1984, one of only six such awards announced nationally that year. Cooperative education placements are open to students of sophomore status or above who have at least a 2.0 cumulative grade point average. Soon the program will expand to include international placements in support of the college's emerging identity as "the college of choice for a global and multicultural education," a theme development importantly supported by a large competitive grant from the State of New Jersey.

Retention. Overall, the four-year student persistence rate at Ramapo hovers somewhat below the national average for colleges of our type and, as a result, is a cause for strong institutional concern. Historically, the retention rate for EOP students has been somewhat low, although not as depressed as some might have expected, given the poor academic backgrounds characteristic of most EOP students.

In striking contrast to both these retention rates, the persistence rate for all Cooperative Education Program participants remains remarkably high at 92 percent. This figure is no doubt inflated in part because cooperative education students are self-selected, have a strong desire to maximize their opportunities, and possess generally better than average academic records. Nevertheless, this tremendous disparity in retention rates was evidence enough that an attempt to link the relatively low-persistence EOP students with the relatively high-retention Cooperative Education Program was found to be worth an investment of time and money.

Funding. In the first year of our Minority Achievement Program, the Cooperative Education Program was awarded a grant by the Association of American Colleges, with funds provided by Sears Roebuck Foundation. With this initial award, a comprehensive career development program was developed for minority students. In its second year, funding for the program was undertaken by the college. This academic year, the project enrolls thirty-six students and is operating with special support from New Jersey's Educational Opportunity Fund Program. The program is coordinated by a Hispanic graduate of Ramapo College under the supervision of the director of cooperative education (the creator of the program). The state of New Jersey, noting its promise for recruitment and retention, recently awarded full funding for its fourth year.

Desired Program Outcomes. As currently configured, the Minority Achievement Program (MAP) is designed to achieve several student successes:

1. Persistence of MAP participants should be greater than that of other EOP students.

2. MAP students should earn higher cumulative grade point averages than nonparticipating EOP students.

3. MAP participants should be more goal-directed and have greater awareness of an appropriate vocational future than EOP nonparticipants.

There are other, secondary objectives: MAP participants should use the college's extensive and formal career development services more than nonparticipants. Successful completion of the MAP program should lead to increased individual self-confidence and poise as well as to greater comfort within the predominantly white environment of the college itself and potential employers. Finally, program participants should graduate from Ramapo College and either find permanent employment commensurate with their personal educational levels or they should enter graduate school.

How MAP Works. Each year, forty sophomore and junior students are selected jointly by counselors working in the Educational Opportunity Program and by the staff of the Cooperative Education Office.

Selected students are those who wish to participate in MAP, but they are not chosen solely because they have demonstrated strong academic performances. Instead, there is a deliberate attempt to include a certain number of academically marginal students, since we know that they are among the most likely to leave college prematurely.

The program itself comprises 26 training sessions and runs through both fall and spring semesters. During the first semester, students concentrate on the self-assessment of interests, values, and skills, as well as analyzing prior academic and work experiences in substantial detail. The Strong-Campbell, the California Occupational Preference System, and the Temperament and Values Inventories are administered and the results individually interpreted for each student. Additionally, each participant uses the SIGI-Plus computerized career guidance system to produce a personal printout concerning his or her values and interests as well as obtaining information about particular career areas and ways to gather more detailed information. The overall goal of the first semester's work is to create in the student the self-knowledge and personal time management skills necessary for academic success and increased goal-directedness.

The second semester's activities are more clearly job-related. Students learn to use the college's career library to discover more about specific occupations and to do in-depth investigations of potential employers of personal interest. They learn to prepare a resume and to perform in both information-interviewing and position-interviewing situations. The development of interviewing skills is specifically accomplished through intensive practice involving the use of audiovisual equipment and an internally developed tape entitled, "An Employer's View of Hiring." Taped interviews with minority professionals active in four areas for which Ramapo prepares substantial numbers of students are also viewed by student participants and are discussed. A live discussion with five Ramapo EOP alumni, called "You Can Do It Too: Finding That First Job," encourages students to recognize that there can be a tangible payoff at the end of what can seem to them at the time a very arduous four years of college. In addition, students visit work sites in northern New Jersey where they view the overall operations, learn more about company organization, and meet with minority professionals employed in specializations of particular personal interest.

The culmination of this rather extensive preparation program is a cooperative education placement during the summer immediately following the conclusion of the twenty-six-week series. At these work sites, students are supervised both by on-site professionals and by faculty members from Ramapo College who actually award the credits earned.

An important additional benefit for Educational Opportunity Program students has been the money earned on these jobs. As national financial aid policies have put more emphasis on the loan aspect of financial aid packaging, minority students have been placed in an increasingly precarious and disadvantageous position. The relatively good wages available through suitable cooperative education placements help to bridge that gap for these students who are also the college's most financially needy. An additional benefit remains the possibility that students completing cooperative education assignments will be offered permanent positions once they graduate—a welcome outcome indeed for many students who fear that, even with a college diploma, they will remain unemployed or underemployed.

Mentoring: A Special Strength of MAP. One of the most vital components of the Minority Achievement Program is the individual mentoring received from working minority professionals. In the past minorities have sometimes lost opportunities with employers because there was no one to whom they could comfortably go for advice, no one to smooth the way. The opportunity to interact with minority professionals is thus a decided plus. Students receive an orientation to an industry and to specific job tasks, and most important, they see someone of similar race and background doing well on the job.

Mentoring gives students the chance to speak with persons who can answer career-related questions, offer personal insights, and provide relevant information about particular jobs. Mentors help students to find out what they do not know and to prepare themselves for career competition in white-dominated organizations.

Minority students are rarely in a position to know people who can "open doors" for them. Professionals who agree to act in the mentor role provide expertise and friendship to students who will be blazing new trails, and they provide a level of comfort they would not have enjoyed otherwise. MAP students report that this aspect of the program is highly rewarding and is an invaluable asset to their total career development.

From the Cooperative Education Office's point of view, the mentoring project is equally rewarding. Of the forty professionals who were approached to permit Ramapo students to spend a day or more with them so that they could gain an insider's view of chosen professions, not one said no. The enthusiastic response and participation of so many mentors was extremely touching and left Ramapo staff members even more motivated to guide MAP students toward success.

The experiences of individual students often led them to important decisions. One student spent a day with an on-camera news reporter from WCBS, running from story to story. She returned to the college utterly exhausted, commenting, "I could never work at that pace." She then promptly switched her career aspirations to student personnel and is currently working on a master's degree at the University of Maryland. It remains to be seen how she will find the pace in student affairs!

Ramapo participants were mentored by professionals at such outstanding firms as J. Walter Thompson, Dancer Fitzgerald Sample, The Record, Essence Magazine, IBM, WCBS, WNBC, Fordham University, the Passaic County Probation Office, Avon, the Internal Revenue Service, the Irving Trust, Levi Strauss, and Sony.

Other students participated in videotaped practice interviews with representatives from Medicomp, Volvo, Lederle Labs, Western Union, and Grandmet. They toured Hewlett Packard, IBM, and the NBC studios, and several students confirmed career choices that, until then, had only been tentative.

Student Success Stories. Most students who participated in the Minority Achievement Program left it better prepared for vocational success. In the view of Ramapo staff members and the students' mentors, program participants at the end were more goal-directed, more self-disciplined, and better informed about entering a world that in far too many cases had heretofore been foreign territory to their families and to their high school contemporaries.

Three short illustrative cases best sum up the impact the Minority Achievement Program has had on individual lives. These are success stories that would not have happened without the assistance the program offered. (The names of all students in the following vignettes have been changed to protect their privacy, but the experiences actually occurred as described.)

Susan. Susan entered Ramapo through the Educational Opportunity Program with poor prospects for success. Not only had she not done well academically in high school, Susan had been a heavy user of illegal drugs there and had what she described as an attitude problem.

Things began to change for Susan at Ramapo. She became interested in psychology and began to earn good grades. She decided to become a psychologist because she credited a teacher's help in high school and the counseling she received in college with her turnaround.

The Minority Achievement Program assigned Susan to a minority therapist who would serve as her mentor. At somewhat the same time, a grant from the college permitted Susan to attend a women's leadership conference in Washington, D.C., at which she met several women active in public life.

The two nearly simultaneous experiences were valuable, ultimately convincing Susan that she no longer wished to become a therapist but instead would turn her talents toward wider audiences. Susan lent her considerable acting talents to a hilarious videotape for the Minority Achievement Program, concerning how not to interview for a job. She became the selected representative to speak on behalf of her class at graduation. Susan helped the college to establish a partnership with her old high school, which will bring more talented minority students to

Ramapo, and she will begin law school in the fall. The Minority Achievement Program helped Susan to sort out her real interests and to make a better-informed choice.

Harold. Despite a fairly severe stuttering problem and poor academic preparation in high school, Harold majored in business administration at Ramapo and was a solid contributor to the football team. Before his participation in the Minority Achievement Program, Harold had poor luck in interviews because of his anxiety-related speech problems, despite job-related skills that were actually quite strong.

Through intensive work using the program's videotaping equipment and with the help of his mentor, Harold's interviewing skills improved so dramatically that he was able to obtain a job as a computer programmer at a Wall Street firm. The program allowed his real talents, which otherwise might not have been observed, to shine through.

Jean. Jean was fortunate to be paired with a black female mentor who is a famous television newscaster in the New York metropolitan area. Jean, a shy student, whose best skills are demonstrated in written, not spoken, words needed the enthusiastic encouragement of this remarkably warm and dynamic mentor. Subsequent to this mentoring experience, Jean became the first EOP student to serve as editor-in-chief of the college newspaper. She won the Dean's Award for Exceptional Service to the College and ultimately obtained a job as an assistant editor with a well-known publisher of business and educational materials in New York City. Jean's career choice in the communications field was thus confirmed by her experiences with her mentor and her work on her cooperative education assignment.

Conclusion. The EOP cooperative education retention initiative is successful not only because it links offices and programs *within* the college but also because it is strengthened by its corporate partnerships that permit students to see more directly the rewards of their academic labors. Grade point averages and retention rates for student participants increase and this, in turn, expands students' options. Minority mentors provide strong role models, and career choices become more focused. Students experience enhanced self-esteem, and this leads to better performance when applying for work and on the job. Successfully placing program participants after graduation provides a whole new generation of mentors.

Advisement Program for High-Risk Adult Students at Canisius College
Esther A. Northman

Canisius College and Its Environment. In the Jesuit tradition, Canisius stresses the study of the liberal arts in every curriculum and has particularly strong programs in the sciences and business. Primarily an undergraduate institution, the college has a coeducational enrollment of approximately 3600 undergraduates (2500 Day Division, 1100 Continuing Studies Division), and 700 graduate students (in the MBA and graduate education programs). Students come primarily from middle-class backgrounds, and 78 percent of Day Division students commute to school, although the resident population has been increasing in the last two years.

The Division of Continuing Studies. Canisius has served adult students since 1919, when it entered the adult education field by offering evening education courses for teachers. In the ensuing years the offerings for evening adult students have fluctuated, depending on the needs of the western New York community. Currently, with the growing demand for adult learning in the 1980s, the Division of Continuing Studies has progressively expanded in size, offerings, and new programs. In the fall 1986 semester, 1097 students enrolled in the Division of Continuing Studies. This figure includes 844 evening students and 253 students in a provisional program for traditional-age students. The high-risk adult learners discussed in this section are included in the evening student category. The typical Canisius adult learner is under thirty-five years old, single, white, and Catholic, but there is a much higher representation of minority and Protestant students than in the traditional-age Canisius population. The majority of adult students hold full-time jobs, are pursuing business majors, and have had some prior higher education.

The Division of Continuing Studies is responsible for virtually all undergraduate and noncredit academic programs that attract adult learners, including: ten bachelor's degrees, two associate's degrees, a special entry program for women and first-time adult students, a portfolio review of noncollegiate learning, audio and video cassette courses for degree credit, three certificate programs of thirty credit hours each, and numerous noncredit special programs for business, government, social, religious, and educational groups.

The college has long recognized that adult learners have different needs and concerns than those of the traditional-age student. Many adult students have resumed their studies after an interruption of several years and lack confidence in their ability to succeed academically. They face the usual pressures of job, home, and school responsibilities, and as new students, they feel uncomfortable in the unfamiliar academic environment. These factors alone would be sufficient to label these students "high risk." Many adult learners are further limited by a lack of adequate academic skills.

The Continuing Studies Division staff believes that good academic advisement especially geared to these high-risk adult students is an important component of their adjustment to college and their pursuit of educational goals. The success of its advisement program is evidenced by the substantial improvement in student retention, which has risen from 20 percent in the 1970s to a current rate of 49 percent (fall 1985 to fall 1986).

The college has given support to the division by increasing its administrative staff, which has tripled in the last five years. Currently, eight administrators staff the division, including the dean, associate dean, and three professional advisers. The Division of Continuing Studies is fortunate in having such a large professional advisement staff to serve its adult learners. The size of the advisement staff is justified as cost effective, since these staff members also advise in the college's program for traditional-age high-risk students.

A member of the advisement staff is available all day Monday through Friday as well as four evenings a week to assist students with any academic problem they encounter. Students are encouraged to see the same adviser regularly to establish a personal rapport, although any adviser can help a student, since detailed advisement notes are kept in the student's academic folder. Advisers can also obtain academic information about all students from their desk-top computers, which access the college's student record system.

Because of the special aspects involved in advising high-risk adult students, the division rigorously trains its new academic advisers. The dean, the associate dean, and the experienced advisers work closely with the new adviser, explaining the unique needs, circumstances, and constraints of adult learners and carefully going over the special advisement strategies to best assist these students. During these advisement training sessions, the new adviser learns the importance of identifying each student's sources of attrition risk. This knowledge will enable the adviser to deal with potential problems before they become serious enough to cause withdrawal from school. After the initial training sessions, all advisers meet frequently during each semester to share student concerns, curriculum changes, and new ideas.

Process of Advisement. Consistent with the philosophy of the Division of Continuing Studies advisement is geared to the individual. When adult learners apply to Canisius College, they meet with a counselor from the Office of Student Recruitment to discuss the college's offerings and services. Canisius is flexible in its admission criteria for adults, since the division carefully assesses its students' academic standing by thorough testing and placement into special development courses. Students with weak academic backgrounds can enter the college with a nonmatriculating status. If they succeed academically as nonmatriculating, they are contacted by an academic adviser and are encouraged to change their status to matriculating. On acceptance to the college, the student is called by a recruitment counselor who notifies the student to make an appointment with a continuing studies academic adviser.

The first advisement session is multifaceted: It is a time for the student to express concerns, questions, and interests to the adviser, who in turn further familiarizes the student with the college's offerings and services. While describing the liberal arts curriculum and discussing possible majors, course options, and transfer credits, the adviser assesses how attrition-prone the student may be by learning about the student's lifestyle, time commitments, and family and work pressures. Since many high-risk students are underprepared academically, the adviser will normally have the student tested in reading, writing, or math. Depending on the test results, the student might be placed in a special academic development course to assist the student in any weak area. Finally, the adviser and student work together to choose a schedule that is consistent with the student's academic goals and individual time constraints. At the end of this important initial advisement session, the adviser strongly encourages the student to remain in contact about any academic concerns and to return for scheduling assistance for the following semester.

A Computerized Progress System. To better track the progress of its high-risk students, the Division of Continuing Studies uses a computer-assisted system that provides advisers with the professor's best estimate of the student's progress and attitude. At midsemester the division sends progress reports to the professors of all new students and students on academic probation (see Figure 1).

The professors respond by filling out a data form for each student, and then they return the completed forms to the Continuing Studies Office. After these reports are received, the advisers contact those students experiencing academic difficulty and arrange a meeting with them. These objective reports on the student's progress bring a much greater precision to the advisement meeting. Time can be devoted to a tough-minded and realistic discussion of the student's progress, conditions for improvement, referrals to tutoring, suggestions for study, and other such options.

Any campus with a computer system and a willing clerical staff can adapt this progress report system. The degree of automation would depend on the sophistication of the computer system, and the success of the program would be contingent on the cooperation of the faculty.

Deficiencies. As a further checkpoint to notify high-risk students of any academic difficulty, the college has instituted a deficiency warning system. Eight weeks into the semester the faculty submits to the registrar the names of students with excessive absences or those doing failing or near-failing work. The registrar then sends these students a deficiency notice that urges them to consult with their academic adviser. One copy of this deficiency form is put in the student's academic folder, and another is sent to the adviser. As in the progress advisement session, the adviser may encourage the student to seek tutoring, to consult with the professor, or if appropriate to withdraw from the course.

Figure 1. Sample Report Form for Student Progress Report

Student
name _____ Course _____ Instructor _____
Spring 1987

PROGRESS REPORTS FOR CONTINUING STUDIES

The purpose of this five-week report is to inform the student of his or her present academic standing and to assist the adviser during the interview.

The purpose of academic advisement is to resolve the problems that students encounter in their first year of college, to improve their academic performance, and to reduce student attrition.

---

(1) Circle the current grade of the student: A B C D F
(2) Circle how you arrived at this grade:
    a. Short quizzes   c. Papers
    b. Hour examinations   d. Classroom discussion
(3) Circle student's attendance record:
    a. Is adequate   b. Needs improving   c. Does not attend at all
(4) Circle appropriate area, if student needs tutoring:
    a. Writing   c. Mathematics
    b. Reading   d. My course
(5) Circle appropriate description(s) of the student's performance:
    a. Works conscientiously and consistently
    b. Is improving
    c. Is doing adequate work but is capable of doing better
    d. Fails to realize demands of college work
    e. Should consult with the instructor
(6) Further comments are welcome:

Academic Disqualification. For those students who do so poorly academically that they are disqualified at the end of the semester, the disqualification process can afford another advisement opportunity. Students who wish to appeal their academic disqualification can meet with the associate dean of continuing studies. At this meeting, if the associate dean deems it appropriate to allow the student to remain in college, he or she will stipulate as a condition for probation that the student meet regularly with an academic adviser who can closely monitor the student's academic progress. Thus, a negative experience can actually have a positive outcome as the student works to improve academic performance with the guidance of the academic adviser.

Cooperation with the Faculty. Much of the success of the advisement system is due to the good spirit of cooperation between the division and the faculty. Throughout the semester faculty members contact the continuing studies advisers to notify them of students with too many absences or deteriorating grades. The division has devised a special form for these situations, which it distributes at the beginning of each semester to all faculty members teaching adult learners. On receiving this form or notification from a faculty member, the adviser contacts the student to set up an advisement appointment to discuss the problem.

Follow-Up Advisement. Effective follow-up advisement is as essential for the retention of high-risk adult students as the initial session. The concern, care, and interest shown by the adviser will determine the student's willingness to seek future advisement. All continuing studies students are strongly encouraged to meet with an adviser each semester for help with their course selection. While it is preferable for students to schedule an individualized advisement appointment with their regular adviser during peak registration periods, special open advisement evenings are scheduled when students may meet without an appointment with advisers (including specially trained faculty members). Those students who choose to be advised at an open advisement evening are urged to return at a later date to meet with one of the professional advisers to go over their curriculum in greater detail. Additionally, the advisers reinforce the importance to the adult learner of returning each semester for follow-up advisement as well as during the semester if any academic problems arise.

The availability and desirability of academic advisement are widely publicized to the adult learners. Prior to registration for the next semester, the dean of continuing studies sends a personalized letter to all students, reminding them to seek academic advisement before registering. Other methods of publicizing advisement include an announcement in the evening student newspaper, notices on the division's electronic bulletin board, which is centrally located in the main classroom building, and encouragement from other students.

Shortly before the new semester begins, a phone retention campaign is conducted by the continuing studies staff, who again encourage continuing students to make an advisement appointment. Another important benefit of the phone retention campaign is the opportunity for the continuing studies staff to learn more about the individual needs of its adult learners as well as the reasons certain students decide to end their studies at Canisius College.

Coordination with Other Offices and Departments. In an effort to help its high-risk adult learners, the continuing studies staff works closely with many other offices and departments on campus. All academic departments that offer majors to evening students request these students to meet at least once a year with a faculty member in their chosen field to discuss their curriculum and as well as job opportunities. The department chairpersons help keep the continuing studies advisers informed of any changes in curriculum and are often present themselves at the open advisement evenings to meet with individual students in their major. The continuing studies advisers assist those students who have not yet declared a major and often refer them to a counselor in the Career Planning Office, which is open two evenings a week to better serve the adult learners. For those adult students experiencing financial difficulties or loss of employment, both of which can be sources of attrition risk, the Career Planning Office offers a complete posting of part-time and full-time jobs. Other special services of the Career Planning Office include evening workshops on resumé writing, interviewing, and job searching, as well as individualized testing to assist in career exploration.

Depending on the specific needs of a student, the adviser may make a direct referral to any of the college services, most of which provide evening hours to serve the adult students. The Counseling Center is particularly sensitive to the needs of high-risk learners. Since the professional counselors on its staff have experience working with adults, they relate well to these students and are able to deal with their specific problems. Early intervention by the Counseling Center is often helpful in retaining high-risk students.

The Academic Development Center cooperates closely with the continuing studies advisement staff to especially assist its high-risk adult learners. This office tests all new students and offers recommendations for placement in its special developmental reading, writing, study-skills, and mathematics courses. The Academic Development Center staff communicates frequently with continuing studies advisers to help adapt these courses to the students' individual needs as well as to inform the advisers of the progress of those students enrolled in their courses. Another important service provided by the Academic Development Office is a comprehensive tutoring program staffed by trained student tutors and part-time faculty. Tutoring is available Monday through Friday as well as four evenings a week in almost all subjects. If a student needs help in a subject for which tutoring is not available, the director of academic development finds an appropriate tutor for that area. Although the continuing studies advisers make direct referrals to tutoring for individual students, many adult students take the initiative themselves. The Continuing Studies Division widely publicizes the availability of tutoring and each semester distributes a list of the tutoring schedule for all courses.

Other Opportunities and Services for Adult Learners. An integral part of the advisement process is assisting the student to adjust to college and adopt a sense of belonging. The Division of Continuing Studies has encouraged the establishment and expansion of two social groups for adult learners. The Encore Club is geared to those adult students who attend classes primarily during the day, while the ESA (Evening Student Association) attracts those students who attend evening classes. Both organizations sponsor many social and educational activities that attract adult learners and help them feel comfortable and actively involved in the college. Since the faculty and advisers often attend these activities, the students have an opportunity to get to know them in a more casual, informal setting. The friendship that is shared by students at these gatherings creates a supportive environment for learning and adds to the students' positive college experience.

To further help high-risk adult learners adapt to Canisius College and ease their concerns about the unknown, the Division of Continuing Studies has developed two special courses. Offered in the evening, one course is an adult freshman seminar that serves as an introduction to college learning as well as being an orientation to Canisius College. The other course, "Perspective on Women," is offered seminar-style one morning per week and is especially geared toward the homemaker who is considering returning to college to prepare herself for the workforce. To maintain a comfortable, personal atmosphere, the size of both courses is kept small, and faculty members are selected who can identify the needs of these students and assist them in their adjustment to college. The continuing studies advisers recommend these courses to those high-risk students they feel would benefit most from them.

Continuing studies advisement has become an invaluable component in assisting its high-risk adult students. Approximately three quarters of all its adult learners seek academic advisement each semester, and that number continues to grow as more students become aware of its value. The development and refinement of the continuing studies advisement system have been major factors in the dramatic improvement in retention of these high-risk students in recent years.

The division has benefited from the faculty's spirit of cooperation, which can be cultivated in a small, private, undergraduate college. Not all colleges are as fortunate as Canisius to have a faculty willing to spend extra time and energy filling out progress forms and contacting academic advisers. Even so, the basic process of advisement for high-risk adult learners at Canisius can easily be replicated. Personnel expenses for advisers and clerical support are the major costs, but a substantial improvement in the retention of these high-risk adult students can justify these expenditures.

Commuter Peer Assistance Program
Allison Liebman, Brent Steele

At colleges and universities across the country, attrition is higher for commuting than for resident students. Studies (Chickering, 1974; Astin, 1980; Beal and Noel, 1980; Noel and others, 1985) suggest that commuting students are high attrition risks because they typically make less of a commitment to attending and continuing college. Residential student persistence is often greater because the decision to pursue a college education has been made, professional or employment goals have been set, college resources are more convenient, financial support is available, and social integration is more inherent. Commuting students are the anomalies, while resident are the norm (Knefelkamp and Stewart, 1983).

In a comprehensive residence program, opportunities for social integration are, for example, much greater than those afforded a commuter student, and this serves to improve a resident's chances of attaining a degree in four years (Astin, 1973). Other than the natural forces encouraging social integration in residence halls, it is the resident assistants who are instrumental in bringing students into closer contact with each other and the campus environment. Also, Upcraft, Peterson, and Moore (1981) have found that the relationship with resident assistants has a positive impact on academic success. Upcraft (1985) also points out that resident assistants have direct responsibility for creating a good living environment. Resident assistants are campus ambassadors; information agents; group facilitators; social, recreation, and cultural program initiators; educational advisers; rules and regulation interpreters and enforcers; and managers of a quiet and safe environment. They do a lot to help students feel connected to the campus, and they provide a strong support system.

To bring the advantages of a resident assistance program to commuters, the Commuter Peer Assistance Program is being piloted at the University of Maryland–Baltimore County (UMBC). This program recognizes the discrete difference between residents and commuter populations and their respective environments and services. It removes the discipline maintenance and management components of resident life, and the program builds on the mentoring concept as an approach to assisting commuting students. The Commuter Peer Assistance Program is simply one effort to increase the retention of commuting students and help them identify quickly with the university, its resources, and its activities. It involves small groups of randomly selected new students, who meet weekly for very specific purposes.

General Description. The Commuter Peer Assistance Program was initiated in 1984 as a pilot program. At that time data from the Academic Leave and Withdrawal Office pointed to a higher attrition rate among commuting students than resident students. The population of UMBC consists of 78 percent commuting students. This disproportionately high attrition rate among commuters reflected national trends and therefore was not surprising. In addition, little was known about what specific factors were operating on the campus to influence this attrition.

Retention studies support the need for social integration of commuters on campus. Involvement in campus activities provides this obvious advantage. However, the results of a campus needs assessment conducted by the Office of Commuter Affairs point to a desire among commuters to participate in campus activities, but personal time commitment block this involvement. The Commuter Peer Assistance Program was created as a retention intervention designed to facilitate social integration and ultimately to increase the persistence of freshman commuting students. The goals of the program are as follows:

- Provide identifiable and accessible support to commuting freshmen
- Offer information and referrals that the students might otherwise have to seek out
- Provide opportunities for freshmen to meet other freshmen
- Provide opportunities for freshmen to interact with professors
- Promote involvement in campus life
- Encourage and support academic success.

The Process. One upperclass student was chosen to be the commuter assistant (CA). A standard hiring process began in July 1985. The CA position was posted in the Career Development and Placement Office, and an invitation to apply was extended to all student peer advisers (peer assistants for orientation). A flyer was also circulated around the campus, and a stipend of $500 was offered.

Fifty freshmen were chosen randomly from students who attended orientation. The freshman participants were randomly assigned through use of the roster of admitted students who were scheduled for orientation. The date of the freshman orientation was irrelevant to the selection. The only contact made with the control group was through a survey of involvement and interest in campus activities, which was administered in December.

The active participants received a letter describing the Commuter Peer Assistance Program and encouraging their involvement. The students were given the name of their CA and a description of the program. The fact that participation was not mandatory was addressed, and freshmen were given a date, location, and time of the first group meeting.

Those who designed the program feel that the most important role of the CA is to make the initial contact with freshmen and to identify himself or herself as an *ongoing support person*. The freshmen are made aware of the hours the CA is available and where to find him or her. In addition to the structured hours, the CA often tells the freshmen where he or she takes meals and socializes on campus so informal contacts can be pursued.

The CA is a *resource and referral source* for the commuting freshmen. Early in the semester, freshmen need many types of information (Wilmes and Quade, 1986). The CA often mails out tip sheets and organizes resource lists, in anticipation of the concerns of the freshmen. Examples of these include study tips for finals, instructions for tutorial services, and information about advising and registration. As time passes the commuter assistant adopts the role of *peer adviser* to the freshmen. Freshmen will often approach the CA for advice with academic or personal concerns or questions. The CA assists the student in problem solving and offers encouragement.

The CA is also a *programmer.* He or she is required to produce one program per month for the group. The CA often bases the programs on needs expressed by individuals within the group. Programs range from video parties and trips to Washington, D.C., to time management or study-skills seminars. In addition, the CA may join students in attending a Greek organization rush or campus event.

Program Effectiveness. The program appears to be a success in many ways. The grade point average and persistence of the freshmen in the treatment and control groups from the pilot study were compared, and significant differences were revealed. Of those in the active group, four students had dropped out by their sophomore year. One of these persons appeared to have academic problems. In the control group, fourteen students had dropped out, seven of whom were academically dismissed, and four whose grade point averages were below 1.8. The average GPA for the active group was 2.68, and the average GPA for the control group was 2.03.

One of the students in the active group went on to become the president of the Commuting Student Association. Many commuters never attended a single meeting. However, the CA communicated by telephone or mail with each student. Conventional programs that require students to meet together are often minimally successful, as they become just another obligation competing for the commuting students' time. Creative programming that allows for interaction, without requiring it, will be most successful. The CA was more effective in reaching the commuting freshmen with information on how to join in established campus activities, and in furnishing information through the mail that the student might have received in a workshop, than in planning a meeting.

The program proved successful enough to repeat and expand in the following year, hiring four commuter assistants and reaching two hundred commuting freshmen. Each CA now receives a $250 stipend, three credits, and a grade per semester.

Some patterns were noted during both years of the program, and they may be useful to consider in future planning. By the end of the first semester, the freshmen are less interested in maintaining a relationship with the CA. As a result, the CAs can take on projects to assist the Office of Commuter Affairs in reaching the broader commuter population. Another pattern observed was involvement in the CA program by freshmen who were not selected into the groups. The program only reaches two hundred of approximately eleven hundred commuting freshmen. Friends of some of the freshmen in the groups want to become involved and are often included in activities. Sufficient resources are necessary to create an equitable program. However, piloting the program with very little financial support proved to be a successful strategy in establishing its value. Finally, the commuting freshmen are very pleased with the program. The freshmen were reluctant to return evaluations, but those returned indicate that students found the program enjoyable and educational.

As additional data are collected, the effective components of the program will become more visible. The experience thus far has been rewarding and encouraging. From general feedback received, the key components seem to be the attention and recognition the commuter receives during the first weeks after entering the university; the identification with the university, which begins when the freshmen clarify their role on campus through membership in the CA group; and the accessible academic and personal support the CA has to offer.

The concept of peer assistance advocated here is not new; neither is the student mentoring function for freshmen that CAs perform. It is important to note the advantage this attention and support can offer, specifically to commuting students. A commuter assistant wrote in her final paper, "If [this] was established as a traditional freshman experience, I truly believe students would feel a deep bond of commitment to UMBC in response to the individual attention and caring they would receive from their CA."

References

Astin, A. W. "The Impact of Dormitory Living on Students." *Educational Record,* 1973, *54*, 204–210.

Astin, A. W. *The American Freshman: National Norms for Fall 1980.* Washington, D.C.: American Council on Education and the University of California, Los Angeles, 1980.

Beal, P. E., and Noel, L. *What Works in Student Retention.* Iowa City, Iowa: American College Testing Program and National Center for Higher Education Management Systems, 1980.

Chickering, A. W. *Commuting Versus Resident Students: Overcoming the Educational Inequities of Living Off Campus.* San Francisco: Jossey-Bass, 1974.

Ewell, P. T. *Conducting Student Retention Studies.* Boulder, Colo.: National Center for Higher Education Management Systems (NCHEMS), 1984.

Hodgkinson, H. L. *All One System: Demographics of Education, Kindergarten Through Graduate School.* Washington, D.C.: Institute for Educational Leadership, 1985.

Knefelkemp, L., and Stewart, S. S. "Toward a New Conceptualization of Commuter Student: The Developmental Perspective." In S. S. Stewart (ed.), *Commuter Students: Enhancing Their Educational Experiences.* New Directions for Student Services, no. 24. San Francisco: Jossey-Bass, 1983.

Noel, L., Levitz, R., and Saluri, D. (eds.). *Increasing Student Retention: Effective Programs and Practices for Reducing the Dropout Rate.* San Francisco: Jossey-Bass, 1985.

Upcraft, M. L. "Residence Halls and Student Activities." In L. Noel, R. Levitz, and D. Saluri (eds.). *Increasing Student Retention: Effective Programs and Practices for Reducing the Dropout Rate.* San Francisco: Jossey-Bass, 1985.

Upcraft, M. L., Peterson, P. C., and Moore, B. L. "The Academic and Personal Development of Penn State Freshmen." Published manuscript, Residence Life Programs, Pennsylvania State University, 1981.

Wilmes, M. B., and Quade, S. L. "Perspectives on Programming for Commuters: Examples of Good Practice." *NASPA Journal,* 1986, *24,* 25–35.

Stuart J. Sharkey is vice-president for student affairs at the University of Delaware.

Pamela M. Bischoff is dean of students, Ramapo College.

Dorothy Echols is director of cooperative education at Ramapo College.

Carol Morrison is associate director of cooperative education at Ramapo College of New Jersey.

Esther A. Northman is an academic adviser at Canisius College.

Allison Liebman is director of commuter affairs at University of Maryland, Baltimore County.

Brent Steele is assistant vice-chancellor for student affairs at University of Maryland, Baltimore County.

The benefits of a consortium are potentially enormous, but care must be taken in its design, budgeting, and implementation.

The Benefits of Consortium Participation

William M. Klepper, Martha McGinty Stodt

At the outset, the values to be gained from participating in the consortium seemed self-evident, and the outcomes do appear to validate our expectations. Before we examine the benefits of the consortium, however, a few caveats:

Do's and Don't's

Consortium Funding. The operation of a consortium requires funds explicitly designated for that purpose. Participating institutions may absorb costs such as their own telephone and secretarial services, but travel to consortium meetings and expenses for consultants must be added to each institution's budget. In addition, a successful consortium needs a central person to coordinate activities, communicate with members, and perform various administrative functions. Also a professional with both academic and administrative credentials, who is qualified to consult with campuses about student needs, learning theory, and retention, is essential to the vitality of a consortium. In our experience, the fact that one person enacted these two roles provided cohesion to the efforts of the consortium. These two basic roles of director and consultant are time consuming, of

M. M. Stodt, W. M. Klepper (eds.). *Increasing Retention: Academic and Student Affairs Administrators in Partnership.*
New Directions for Higher Education, no. 60. San Francisco: Jossey-Bass, Winter 1987.

course, and require compensation. We recognized that we were inadequately funded but felt that the consortium would not "get off the ground" if it were perceived as expensive. As a result, compensation was minimal, host institutions for meetings bore extraordinary expense, some representatives could not attend consortium meetings, and occasionally participants incurred personal expense. Moreover, the participating institutions would have benefited from additional support from the director-consultant—through mail, telephone, personal visits—if time could have been provided.

Authority. A consortium's efforts require a considerable amount of legitimacy within the institution in order to be effective. In our enterprise any response to on-campus strategies and any cooperation with consortium suggestions was purely volitional. Our consortium consultant had to establish credibility and earn her authority by performance on campus. An annual visit for two years offered certain benefits, but it lacked the power of follow-through and implementation. Clearly, more interaction was needed. Perhaps institutions considering the formation of a consortium would benefit from negotiating a contract among themselves that would give more implicit authority to the individuals representing the consortium on campus and to its leaders as well. However, it is probably inevitable that the consortium must simply "legitimize" itself by the efficacy of its efforts.

An Assessment Context. In order to discover and disseminate the effectiveness of various retention strategies, the plans for deployment of the institution's resources must be developed within a research design. Empirical evidence from a group of schools would be even more definitive, of course. Toward this end we expended much effort to establish a homogeneous research base, The American Council on Education Cooperative Institutional Research Program (ACE-CIRP). Although all our schools became more advanced in their efforts to develop and use a student data base, the diversity of their methods prohibited any uniform measure of consortium results. In our judgment, a system for assessment should be in place at the outset, and participating institutions should commit themselves to this methodology as they form the consortium.

Adequate Time Span. The length of time institutions agree to commit to a consortium should be sufficient to produce outcomes that are significant. Our consortium was launched in early winter and was to conclude in late spring of the following academic year, essentially one and a half years later. Accordingly, our retention strategies and results turned out to be exploratory—even though they have provided useful information. In our opinion, the minimum time frame for a meaningful measure of an entering freshman cohort would be three years, and four would be much better. Naturally the more one is studying attitude and behavior change, the more time is needed.

Consortium Advantages

After the designated period of the consortium's existence was completed, representatives of the participating schools received a questionnaire. It was based on the benefits we had projected for institutions engaging in the group's activities. The questionnaire items with their mode of response and a summary of comments follow (Rating scale: a. high b. medium c. low d. none e. can't rate):

Please rate the value to you of having communicated with other schools in the consortium regarding your student development and retention efforts:

a. __X__ b. _____ c. _____ d. _____ e. _____

Participants were very enthusiastic about this aspect of the consortium but felt that it should have been extended to more communication outside of meetings. A newsletter to keep members current and increase the sharing of programs, problems, and ideas would have been welcome.

Please rate the value to you of having exchanged ideas, materials, problems, and "success stories" with other schools in the consortium:

a. __X__ b. _____ c. _____ d. _____ e. _____

Respondents found it "very therapeutic" to know that other schools had similar problems. Membership was morale-building. Successful programs at other schools served as models, but in some instances representatives noted difficulty in implementing similar programs due to "campus politics."

Please rate the value to you of having used Astin's worksheet for the fall 1984 entering student class to predict the probability of their dropping out:

a. _____ b. _____ c. __X__ d. _____ e. _____

This rating illustrates the consortium's problem in achieving uniform research measures. A few schools found their in-house predictions to be very satisfactory and were reluctant to change or add another instrument. In some schools institutional research staff members were either unwilling or unequipped to cooperate. When the worksheet was utilized correctly, it was effective.

Please rate the success you had in implementing a campus research program that includes the systematic collection of information on student characteristics and the efficacy of your school's student development and retention efforts:

a. _____ b. __X__ c. _____ d. _____ e. _____

The institutional research offices of a number of the consortium schools had already begun a campus research program and done a good deal with student characteristics. The additional support from the consortium allowed the schools to plug in a student development component.

Please rate the success you had in launching a retention team on your campus from the academic and student affairs areas and getting different branches and programs to cooperate:
a. __X__ b. _____ c. _____ d. _____ e. _____

This was one of the most important areas for the schools to be successful in. The partnership of the academic and student affairs areas was crucial to the development of an effective retention team.

Please rate the success you have had in improving communication on your campus regarding retention, for example, written goals and outcomes:
a. _____ b. __X__ c. _____ d. _____ e. _____

Some schools were able to develop specific goals for reducing attrition, while others wanted retention to become a number-one goal in their long-range planning. The consortium helped to stimulate greater campus communication and raise awareness about retention.

Please rate the success you have had in enlisting your chief executive officer (CEO) and other key administrators' support of the combined goals of quality education, student development, and retention:
a. _____ b. __X__ c. _____ d. _____ e. _____

The visits to the campuses by the director-consultant included discussions with the CEO and other key administrators, which evidenced an understanding and support for the goals of the consortium effort. Harold W. Eickhoff, president of Trenton State College, hosted a two-day meeting of presidents with their chief academic and student affairs officers at the beginning of the second year of the consortium to provide additional momentum to the project.

Please rate the success you have had in identifying those students who are "at risk," and designing and implementing retention strategies for them:
a. _____ b. __X__ c. _____ d. _____ e. _____

Some institutions reported that they had achieved the ability to identify at-risk students and to design strategies to encourage their persistence. They were encountering more difficulty with implementation, monitoring, and evaluation of their retention tactics. Almost all consortium schools had expended some kind of effort at this process, but success varied considerably among the schools.

Please rate the success you have had in identifying the programs and services at your school that are effective or defective in relation to student development and retention:
a. _____ b. __X__ c. _____ d. _____ e. _____

Comments suggested that attempts to identify strengths and weaknesses within the institution had revealed so many defective areas that it clearly required "task force" effort to address correction. Other comments indicated that some colleges were focusing on areas of strength rather than trying to eradicate all the defective areas. Clearly, institutions had become more self-aware regarding their status in relation to meeting students' needs.

Please rate the success you have had in demonstrating on your campus the congruence between programs and practices that promote quality education, student development, and retention:
a. _____ b. _X_ c. _____ d. _____ e. _____

Respondents reported that they were emphasizing quality education as the major component of retention, and they were making progress in increasing institutional awareness of the congruence between educational excellence and retention. On some campuses they perceived less readiness to acknowledge the importance of student development.

Please rate the value to you of using the entering students' questionnaire to gather data for your retention efforts:
a. _X_ b. _____ c. _____ d. _____ e. _____

The schools that participated in the survey of their entering freshmen have found the data to be highly valuable as a means of informing the faculty and staff of the characteristics of their students. When these data are matched with follow-up survey data collected two and four years later, it is possible to make an empirical measurement of the impact of the retention strategies.

Please rate the consortium's consultant in the following areas: creating incentives for bringing together (personnel and program) the campus retention plan from the academic and student affairs areas:
a. _X_ b. _____ c. _____ d. _____ e. _____
preparing and distributing reports that revealed strengths and weaknesses in the school's programs and services:
a. _____ b. _X_ c. _____ d. _____ e. _____
improving the campus practices by sharing her expertise in higher education, the literature, and materials among participating schools:
a. _____ b. _X_ c. _____ d. _____ e. _____
instilling enthusiasm by recognizing and publicizing the school's efforts:
a. _X_ b. _____ c. _____ d. _____ e. _____
acting as a catalyst in removing obstacles:
a. _____ b. _X_ c. _____ d. _____ e. _____

Comments described the consultant as "an enthusiastic and astute consultant, able to read personnel and program problems clearly." In some instances representatives felt that the benefit of her "talents" was reduced by lack of follow-through on the part of the administration.

Please rate the overall value of the consortium to you and comment specifically on the pitfalls that you experienced:
a. __X__ b. _____ c. _____ d. _____ e. _____

In general respondents expressed a high regard for the consortium experience. They valued it personally for the "collegiality and student development research base that it provided." On behalf of their institutions they regretted that the consortium did not provide even more interaction with the consultant and with other schools. They felt that further progress depended on overcoming resistance by key personnel and power figures on campus to new ideas and practices, and they accepted as a challenge that "patience is required due to the slow pace of change and progress."

In summary, we believe that the year-and-a-half consortium experience provided an impetus for each institution's retention efforts progress, examining a school's attitude and efforts toward retention, increasing cooperation among different branches within the institution, setting goals in writing and communicating outcomes, and enlisting more support by the chief executive and other key administrators for the goals of quality education, student development, and retention. The degree to which these effects were achieved varied, of course, from school to school.

The director of the consortium served as an ongoing consultant to the institutions and proved to be valuable as an "outside" expert who knew higher education and its literature, had information about other schools, and could critique and advise. Her follow-up letters after campus visits, discussing strengths and weaknesses of the institution's programs and services, could be utilized as a barometer for future references. Perhaps most important was the "glue" provided to the twelve schools by this role and its functions. Because the consultant had come from academic ranks and had had previous experience as a chief student affairs officer, her credibility quotient was high.

Another benefit received by the consortium schools was institutional recognition from the consortium publicity in professional periodicals as well as the national press. This may have helped motivate the schools to continue their efforts.

The central purpose of the consortium was to bring the academic, administrative, and student affairs staff and program elements together in an effort to improve students' educational experience and encourage their persistence. The campus visits by the consultants focused on the theme of partnership for excellence—and collaboration happened at least in the microcosm of those occasions. In some institutions collegiality was already healthy and flourished in the consortium enterprise. In others the process existed and was nourished by our efforts. In a few institutions the consortium assisted at the birth of an institutional partnership to strive for educational excellence with retention as a derivative.

The Future

At the consortium's final meeting in June 1986, the participants expressed reluctance to disband. Eight of the original twelve schools subsequently formed the East Coast Consortium and have extended membership to other eastern institutions. The structure changed in that the consortium now has no director or central consultant. The members are available to one another for consultation, however, and the group's activities are coordinated by the chief student affairs officer, strongly supported by the chief academic officer of a consortium school. The contact for the East Coast Consortium is Dr. Thomas E. Miller, Canisius College, Buffalo, NY 14208.

In its new format consortium representatives have continued the semiannual meetings to discuss the success of their retention strategies. The coordinator informs the institutions about developments pertaining to the consortium and the individual campuses. Bibliographies, program designs, and retention literature are shared and are available to other institutions on request. Individuals who have gained expertise in specific areas, such as minority student retention, freshman seminars, or retention research, exchange services with colleagues in other schools. A clearinghouse on retention programs has been initiated.

The current status of the consortium seems to be a natural and healthy outgrowth of the original enterprise. Surely the institutions involved can only benefit from this kind of dedicated, responsible endeavor.

William M. Klepper is dean of student life at Trenton State College and has served as a codirector of the consortium in its second year.

Martha McGinty Stodt is adjunct professor of business at Columbia University Graduate School of Business and was director of the Intentional Student Development and Retention Consortium.

Index

1. TITLE OF PUBLICATION	1A. PUBLICATION NO.							2. DATE OF FILING
New Directions for Higher Education	9	9	0	–	8	8	0	10/7/87

3. FREQUENCY OF ISSUE	3A. NO. OF ISSUES PUBLISHED ANNUALLY	3B. ANNUAL SUBSCRIPTION PRICE
quarterly	4	$36 indiv/$48 inst

4. COMPLETE MAILING ADDRESS OF KNOWN OFFICE OF PUBLICATION *(Street, City, County, State and ZIP Code) (Not printers)*

433 California St., San Francisco, San Francisco county, CA 94104

5. COMPLETE MAILING ADDRESS OF THE HEADQUARTERS OR GENERAL BUSINESS OFFICES OF THE PUBLISHERS *(Not printers)*

433 California St., San Francisco, San Francisco county, CA 94104

6. FULL NAMES AND COMPLETE MAILING ADDRESS OF PUBLISHER, EDITOR, AND MANAGING EDITOR *(This item MUST NOT be blank)*

PUBLISHER *(Name and Complete Mailing Address)*

Jossey-Bass Inc., Publishers, 433 California St., San Francisco CA 94104

EDITOR *(Name and Complete Mailing Address)*

Martin Kramer, 2807 Shasta Rd., Berkeley CA 94708

MANAGING EDITOR *(Name and Complete Mailing Address)*

Allen Jossey-Bass, Jossey-Bass Publishers, 433 California St., SF CA 94104

7. OWNER *(If owned by a corporation, its name and address must be stated and also immediately thereunder the names and addresses of stockholders owning or holding 1 percent or more of total amount of stock. If not owned by a corporation, the names and addresses of the individual owners must be given. If owned by a partnership or other unincorporated firm, its name and address, as well as that of each individual must be given. If the publication is published by a nonprofit organization, its name and address must be stated.) (Item must be completed.)*

FULL NAME	COMPLETE MAILING ADDRESS
Jossey-Bass Inc., Publishers	433 California St., SF CA 94104
for names and addresses of stockholders, see attached list	

8. KNOWN BONDHOLDERS, MORTGAGEES AND OTHER SECURITY HOLDERS OWNING OR HOLDING 1 PERCENT OR MORE OF TOTAL AMOUNT OF BONDS, MORTGAGES OR OTHER SECURITIES *(If there are none, so state)*

FULL NAME	COMPLETE MAILING ADDRESS
same as #7	

9. FOR COMPLETION BY NONPROFIT ORGANIZATIONS AUTHORIZED TO MAIL AT SPECIAL RATES *(Section 411.3, DMM only)*
The purpose, function, and nonprofit status of this organization and the exempt status for Federal income tax purposes *(Check one)*

☐ (1) HAS NOT CHANGED DURING PRECEDING 12 MONTHS ☐ (2) HAS CHANGED DURING PRECEDING 12 MONTHS *(If changed, publisher must submit explanation of change with this statement.)*

10. EXTENT AND NATURE OF CIRCULATION	AVERAGE NO. COPIES EACH ISSUE DURING PRECEDING 12 MONTHS	ACTUAL NO. COPIES OF SINGLE ISSUE PUBLISHED NEAREST TO FILING DATE
A. TOTAL NO. COPIES *(Net Press Run)*	1900	3074
B. PAID CIRCULATION 1. SALES THROUGH DEALERS AND CARRIERS, STREET VENDORS AND COUNTER SALES	428	1059
2. MAIL SUBSCRIPTION	937	931
C. TOTAL PAID CIRCULATION *(Sum of 10B1 and 10B2)*	1365	1990
D. FREE DISTRIBUTION BY MAIL, CARRIER OR OTHER MEANS SAMPLES, COMPLIMENTARY, AND OTHER FREE COPIES	88	140
E. TOTAL DISTRIBUTION *(Sum of C and D)*	1453	2130
F. COPIES NOT DISTRIBUTED 1. OFFICE USE, LEFT OVER, UNACCOUNTED, SPOILED AFTER PRINTING	447	944
2. RETURN FROM NEWS AGENTS		
G. TOTAL *(Sum of E, F1 and 2 – should equal net press run shown in A)*	1900	3074

11. I certify that the statements made by me above are correct and complete	SIGNATURE AND TITLE OF EDITOR, PUBLISHER, BUSINESS MANAGER, OR OWNER *(signature)* Vice-President

PS Form 3526, June 1985

(See instructions on reverse)

(Page 1)